Lecture Notes in Computer Science 16159

Founding Editors

Gerhard Goos
Juris Hartmanis

AF167452

The series Lecture Notes in Computer Science (LNCS), including its subseries Lecture Notes in Artificial Intelligence (LNAI) and Lecture Notes in Bioinformatics (LNBI), has established itself as a medium for the publication of new developments in computer science and information technology research, teaching, and education.

LNCS enjoys close cooperation with the computer science R & D community, the series counts many renowned academics among its volume editors and paper authors, and collaborates with prestigious societies. Its mission is to serve this international community by providing an invaluable service, mainly focused on the publication of conference and workshop proceedings and postproceedings. LNCS commenced publication in 1973.

Shiping Chen · Jun Feng · Yinbin Miao ·
Liang-Jie Zhang

Editors

Metaverse – METAVERSE 2025

21st International Conference
Held as Part of the Services Conference Federation, SCF 2025
Hong Kong, China, September 27–30, 2025
Proceedings

 Springer

Editors
Shiping Chen
UCSIRO Data61
Canberra, TAS, Australia

University of New South Wales
Kensington, Australia

Yinbin Miao
Xidian University
Xi'an, China

Jun Feng 🆔
Huazhong University of Science
and Technology
Wuhan, China

Liang-Jie Zhang 🆔
Shenzhen University
Shenzhen, China

ISSN 0302-9743   ISSN 1611-3349 (electronic)
Lecture Notes in Computer Science
ISBN 978-3-032-06322-9   ISBN 978-3-032-06323-6 (eBook)
https://doi.org/10.1007/978-3-032-06323-6

This Springer imprint is published by the registered company Springer Nature Switzerland AG
The registered company address is: Gewerbestrasse 11, 6330 Cham, Switzerland

If disposing of this product, please recycle the paper.

Preface

To rapidly respond to the changing economy, the World Congress on Services has been naturally extended to become the International Conference on Metaverse to cover immersive services for all vertical industries and area solutions. With the emergence of Metaverse, the current services will be gradually transformed into immersive services that construct digital worlds and connect with physical worlds. The immersive services are the core characteristics of Metaverse.

METAVERSE 2025 was a member of the Services Conference Federation (SCF). SCF 2025 had the following 10 collocated service-oriented sister conferences: 2025 International Conference on Web Services (ICWS 2025), 2025 International Conference on Cloud Computing (CLOUD 2025), 2025 International Conference on Services Computing (SCC 2025), 2025 International Conference on Big Data (BigData 2025), 2025 International Conference on AI & Multimodal Services (AIMS 2025), 2025 International Conference on Metaverse (METAVERSE 2025), 2025 International Conference on Internet of Things (ICIOT 2025), 2025 International Conference on Cognitive Computing (ICCC 2025), 2025 International Conference on Edge Computing (EDGE 2025), and 2025 International Conference on Blockchain (ICBC 2025).

This volume presents the accepted papers of the 2025 International Conference on Metaverse (METAVERSE 2025), held in Hong Kong, China during September 27–30, 2025. For this conference, each paper was single-blind reviewed by three independent members of the International Program Committee. After carefully evaluating their originality and quality, we accepted 9 papers from 11 submissions.

We are pleased to thank the authors whose submissions and participation made this conference possible. We also want to express our thanks to the Organizing Committee and Program Committee members, for their dedication in helping to organize the conference and reviewing the submissions. We owe special thanks to the keynote speakers for their impressive speeches.

Finally, we would like to thank operations team members Jing Zeng, Sheng He, Yishuang Ning, and Zhuolin Mei for their excellent work in organizing this conference. We look forward to your future great contributions as a volunteer, author, and conference participant in the fast-growing worldwide services innovations community.

August 2025

Shiping Chen
Jun Feng
Yinbin Miao
Liang-Jie Zhang

Organization

Program Chairs

Shiping Chen	CSIRO Data61 & UNSW, Australia
Jun Feng	Huazhong University of Science and Technology, China
Yinbin Miao	Xidian University, China

Application and Industry Track Chairs

Jiacai Lai	Peking University (Tianjin Binhai) New Generation Information Technology Research Institute, China
Tiehua Zhang	Tongji University, China

Services Conference Federation (SCF 2025)

General Chairs

Ali Arsanjani	Google, USA
Wu Chou	Essenlix Corporation, USA

Coordinating Program Chair

Liang-Jie Zhang	Shenzhen University, China

CFO and International Affairs Chair

Min Luo	Services Society, USA

Operation Committee

Jing Zeng	China Gridcom Co., Ltd., China
Yishuang Ning	Tsinghua University, China

Sheng He	Kingdee International Software Group Co., Ltd., China
Zhuolin Mei	Jiujiang University, China

Steering Committee

Calton Pu (Co-chair)	Georgia Tech, USA
Liang-Jie Zhang (Co-chair)	Shenzhen University, China

METAVERSE 2025 Program Committee

Ahmed Berbar	University of Science and Technologies Houari Boumedien, Algeria
Venkata Suman Doma	Deloitte, USA
Xinxin Fan	IoTeX, USA
Abdurazzag A. Aburas	Beykoz University, Turkey
Atheer Alaa Hammad	Ministry of Education, Iraq
Ben Falchuk	Peraton Labs, USA
Ge Wang	Xi'an Jiaotong University, China
Kunjing Zhang	Institute of Information and Technology, China
Lijun Li	Guizhou University of Commerce, China
Na Yu	Samsung Research America, USA
Sheng He	Kingdee International Software Group Co., Ltd., China
Artem Barger	Idea Blockchain Research Lab, Israel
Changhao Chenli	Indiana Institute of Technology, USA
Fusang Zhang	Chinese Academy of Sciences, China
Gang Wang	University of Connecticut, USA
Gururaj H. L.	Manipal Institute of Technology Bengaluru, India
Hasan Ali Ali Khattak	National University of Sciences and Technology, Pakistan
Ikbal Taleb	Zayed University, United Arab Emirates
Lei Xu	Kent State University, USA
Pengfei Wang	Dalian University of Technology, China
Stefano Sebastio	Raytheon Technologies, Ireland
Vikas S. Shah	Knights of Columbus, USA
Xiaohu Fan	Wuhan Collage, China

Conference Sponsor – Services Society

The Services Society (S2) is a non-profit professional organization that has been created to promote worldwide research and technical collaboration in services innovations among academia and industrial professionals. Its members are volunteers from industry and academia with common interests. S2 is registered in the USA as a "501(c) organization", which means that it is an American tax-exempt nonprofit organization. S2 collaborates with other professional organizations to sponsor or co-sponsor conferences and to promote an effective services curriculum in colleges and universities. S2 initiates and promotes a "Services University" program worldwide to bridge the gap between industrial needs and university instruction.

The Services Sector accounted for 79.5% of the GDP of the USA in 2016. The Services Society has formed 5 Special Interest Groups (SIGs) to support technology- and domain-specific professional activities.

- Special Interest Group on Services Computing (SIG-SC)
- Special Interest Group on Big Data (SIG-BD)
- Special Interest Group on Cloud Computing (SIG-CLOUD)
- Special Interest Group on Artificial Intelligence (SIG-AI)
- Special Interest Group on Metaverse (SIG-Metaverse)

About the Services Conference Federation (SCF)

As the founding member of the Services Conference Federation (SCF), the first **International Conference on Web Services (ICWS)** was held in June 2003 in Las Vegas, USA. Meanwhile, the First International Conference on Web Services - Europe 2003 (ICWS-Europe 2003) was held in Germany in October 2003. ICWS-Europe 2003 was an extended event of the 2003 International Conference on Web Services (ICWS 2003) in Europe. In 2004, ICWS-Europe was changed to the European Conference on Web Services (ECOWS), which was held in Erfurt, Germany.

Sponsored by the Services Society and Springer, SCF 2018 and SCF 2019 were held successfully on June 25 - June 30, 2018, in Seattle, USA, and on June 25 – June 30, 2019, in San Diego, USA. SCF 2020 and SCF 2021 were held successfully online and in satellite sessions in Shenzhen, China. SCF 2022 and 2023 were held successfully on December 10 - 14, 2022 and on September 23 - 26, 2023, in Hawaii, USA. SCF 2024 was held successfully on November 16 - 19, 2024, in Bangkok, Thailand. To celebrate its 23rd birthday, SCF 2025 was held on September 27-30, 2025, in Hong Kong, China.

In the past 22 years, the ICWS community has expanded from Web engineering innovations to scientific research for the whole services industry. Service delivery platforms have been expanded to mobile platforms, the Internet of Things, cloud computing, and edge computing. The services ecosystem has gradually been enabled, value-added, and intelligence embedded through enabling technologies such as big data, artificial intelligence, and cognitive computing. In the coming years, all transactions with multiple parties involved will be transformed into blockchain and metaverse.

Based on technology trends and best practices in the field, the Services Conference Federation (SCF) will continue serving as the conference umbrella's code name for all services-related conferences. SCF 2025 defined the future of New ABCDE (AI, Blockchain, Cloud, BigData, & IOT) and entered the 5G for Services Era. **The theme of SCF 2025 was Services Agent.** We are very proud to announce that SCF 2025's 10 co-located theme topic conferences all centered around "services", with each focusing on exploring different themes (web-based services, cloud-based services, Big Data-based services, services innovation lifecycle, AI-driven ubiquitous services, blockchain-driven trust service ecosystems, industry-specific services and applications, and emerging service-oriented technologies).

- **Bigger Platform:** The 10 collocated conferences (SCF 2025) were sponsored by the Services Society, which is the world-leading not-for-profit organization (501(c)(3)) dedicated to the service of more than 30,000 worldwide Services Computing researchers and practitioners. A bigger platform means bigger opportunities for all volunteers, authors, and participants. Meanwhile, Springer provided sponsorship of the best paper awards and other professional activities. All the 10 conference proceedings of SCF 2025 were published by Springer and indexed in the ISI Conference

Proceedings Citation Index (included in Web of Science), Engineering Index EI (Compendex and Inspec databases), DBLP, Google Scholar, IO-Port, MathSciNet, Scopus, and ZBlMath.

- **Brighter Future:** While celebrating the 2025 version of ICWS, SCF 2025 highlighted the International Conference on AI and Multimodal Services (AIMS 2025) to build the fundamental infrastructure for enabling AIGC services ecosystems. It will also lead our community members to create their own brighter future.
- **Better Model:** SCF 2025 continued to leverage the invented Conference Blockchain Model (CBM) to innovate the organizing practices for all the 10 theme conferences. Senior researchers in the field are welcome to submit proposals to serve as CBM Ambassador for an individual conference to start better interactions during your leadership role in organizing future SCF conferences.

We look forward to your great contributions as a volunteer, author, and conference participant for the fast-growing worldwide services innovations community. If you would like to contribute to SCF 2026 as a leading volunteer or try the new Conference Blockchain Model, please feel free to contact us to become a conference volunteer. For other queries or questions, please feel free to visit our conference websites and find contact information on SCF 2026.

All the invited talks and paper presentations of SCF 2020, SCF 2021, and SCF 2022 are open to all Services Society community members for free. You can watch all presentations through SCF 365.

Contents

*Avery Hughes, Showkot Hossain, Wenyi Tang, Taeho Jung,
and Changhao Chenli*

A Metaverse-Enabled Immersive Emergency Broadcasting System: Spatial Sensing, Multi-Modal Interaction and Dynamic Adaptation

Ying Song⬤, Xiaohu Fan⬤, Jun Li⬤, and Lingling Wang$^{(\boxtimes)}$ ⬤

Wuhan City Polytechnic, 127# Nanli Road, Wuhan 430072, Hubei, China
{Songying,Fanxiaohu,Lijuntc2000,Wanglingling}@whcp.edu.cn

Abstract. In this paper, we propose a meta-universe-based emergency broadcasting system that integrates digital twin, multi-modal interaction and distributed rendering technologies to address the deficiencies of traditional systems in spatial perception and contextual interaction. The proposed system features a four-layer architecture integrating environment modeling, behavior perception, virtual-reality linkage, and user interaction. By employing digital twin, multimodal interaction, and distributed rendering technologies, the system achieves sub-meter spatial localization, dynamic path planning, and real-time cognitive load optimization. Experimental results demonstrate that the accuracy of the system's information reception is 42% higher than that of the traditional mode, and the emergency response time is shortened to 3.2 s; the multi-modal interaction (AR/VR + haptic feedback) reduces the orientation judgment error by 65.9% and improves the response accuracy of the hearing-impaired and visually-impaired groups by 2.17–2.71 times. The study provides a novel digital paradigm for public safety and advances the practical application of metaverse technology in disaster management.

Keywords: Metaverse · Emergency Broadcasting · Dynamic Path Planning · Cognitive Load Optimization · Federal Kalman Filter

1 Introduction

Recent years have seen frequent extreme weather events globally, with escalating disaster risks [1]. WHO's 2022 report indicates meteorological disasters during 2020–2022 increased by 37.6% compared to the previous decade's average, causing $245 billion annual losses and affecting over 1.8 billion people [2]. Emergency broadcasting systems, as critical 'last-mile' channels, significantly impact evacuation efficiency and damage control [3]. However, traditional systems relying on radio and cellular networks face structural limitations: lack of 3D spatial information, fragmented context-awareness, and inadequate multi-modal interaction [4]. Despite 90% warning coverage, only 60% translates to effective risk avoidance, revealing 'information idling' issues.

© The Author(s), under exclusive license to Springer Nature Switzerland AG 2026
S. Chen et al. (Eds.): METAVERSE 2025, LNCS 16159, pp. 1–14, 2026.
https://doi.org/10.1007/978-3-032-06323-6_1

Metaverse technology offers solutions through digital twins, multi-modal interaction, and distributed rendering, enabling 3D disaster scene reconstruction, real-time coupling, and smart sensing [5]. Existing research demonstrates metaverse potential in emergency management, including AR navigation and AI-optimized broadcasting [6].

This study aims to develop a meta verse-based immersive emergency broadcasting system, addressing: 3D information architecture for spatial perception, multi-modal interaction optimizing cognitive load and decision-making, and quantified effectiveness in disaster response [7]. Focusing on urban disasters (earthquakes, fires), the research utilizes Unity3D and HTC Vive, incorporating Federal Kalman Filter and Edge-Cloud Rendering for large-scale dynamic calibration [8].

Innovations include: a four-layer architecture enabling sub-meter spatial accuracy (RMSE < 0.3 m), a cognitive ergonomics model linking information density (MID) to NASA-TLX scores for real-time optimization, and demonstrated economic feasibility (CBR = 74.6). The results of the study provide theoretical support for digital transformation in the field of public safety and lay the foundation for the engineering landing of meta-universe technology in disaster management.

2   Related Works

Multi-modal interaction technology enhances emergency response through AR/VR and tactile feedback, improving user perception and reaction speed [9]. For instance, smart metro systems use 3D virtual environments to enable efficient communication and remote operations, boosting emergency response effectiveness [10]. While beneficial for information transmission, accessibility especially for hearing and visually impaired users, high equipment costs limit scalability, and multi-modal data fusion remains challenging [11].

The federated Kalman filter algorithm optimizes the accuracy of virtual reality spatial mapping by integrating UWB [12], visual odometer and inertial navigation data, and reduces the spatial mapping error from 1.5 m of the traditional SLAM algorithm to 0.28M [13]. The advantage is that it significantly improves the accuracy of spatial mapping and provides reliable support for emergency path planning. The disadvantage is that the time synchronization requirements of multi-sensor data are high, and the adaptability in complex dynamic environment is insufficient [14].

Recent meta verse-based emergency broadcasting systems leverage digital twins, multi-modal interaction, and edge-cloud rendering to advance spatial awareness and decision-making [15]. Key challenges include computational demands, cost barriers, and reliability in complex scenarios.

3   Architecture and Methods

3.1   System Design

This paper proposes a four-layer virtual-reality linked emergency broadcast architecture. 1) Environment modeling layer: data base layer, through the fusion of BIM and LiDAR point cloud, to generate high-fidelity digital twin of disaster scenes. Provide spatial benchmarks for the upper layer to support the spatial consistency of virtual-reality linkage. 2) Behavior Perception Layer: Cognitive state input layer that collects user physiological data in real time and captures instantaneous behavioral intent through 120Hz sampling rate. The data is input to the virtual-reality linkage layer to adjust the emergency response strategy. 3) Virtual-Real Linkage Layer: the core of spatial synergy, establishing physical-virtual coordinate mapping based on sub-meter calibration of spatial anchors to ensure spatial consistency between rescue instructions and real scenes. 4) User interaction layer: AR/VR terminals providing immersive navigation, haptic feedback devices delivering physical signals such as vibration alarms [16].

The four-layer architecture realizes data closure through distributed rendering and edge computing. After the user triggers an alarm through a haptic device, the digital twin updates the location of the trapped person in real time and recalculates the escape path [17]. The data closure from environment modeling, behavior perception, virtual-reality linkage, user interaction, and environment update is supported. It also builds a complete emergency response chain from disaster sensing, behavioral diagnosis, spatial calibration, and multimodal evacuation instructions (see Fig. 1).

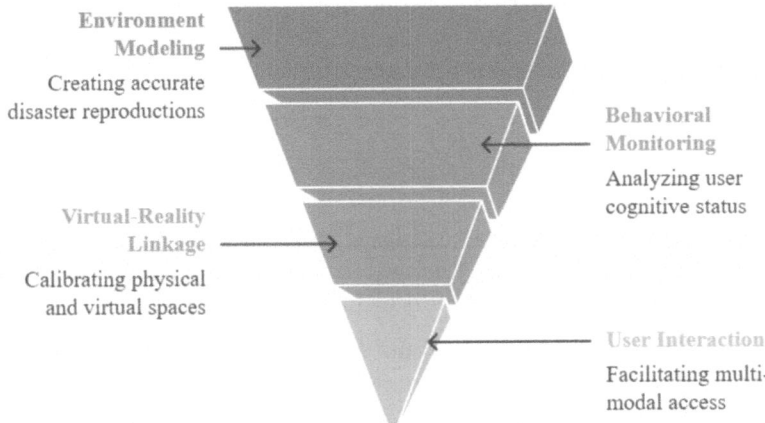

Fig. 1. Overall system architecture diagram

3.2 Core Algorithms

Spatial Sound Field Orientation Algorithm. HRTF (Head Related Transfer Function) is used to achieve 3D audio localization, and the formula (1) is calculated as follows:

$$H(f, \theta, \varphi) = \sum_{n=0}^{N} a_n(f)e^{-j2\pi f \tau_n(\theta,\phi)} \tag{1}$$

where τ_n denotes the difference in time for the sound wave to reach the binaural, and θ, ϕ are the azimuth and elevation angles.

The Complex Exponential Term. It is a common form for representing time delays in the frequency domain and is consistent with the complex exponential decomposition of the Fourier transform. For example, in Discrete Fourier Transform (DFT), the signal is decomposed into a weighted sum of different frequency components, similar to the structure of this formula.

Weighting Coefficients. An (f) can be regarded as frequency-dependent magnitude and phase weights, similar to the coefficients in Fourier series.

Summing Range. Finite summation ($n = 0 \rightarrow N$) indicates that the formula is applicable to discrete systems, unlike the Fourier transform of infinite series.

Array Signal Processing. If τ_n (θ, ϕ) denotes the time delay introduced by the nth array element in the array due to the baud direction(θ, ϕ), then the equation describes the frequency-domain response of beam forming or null-domain filtering.

Multi-path Channel Model. In wireless communication, an (f) and τ_n can represent the fading and propagation delay of the nth path, respectively, when the formula characterizes the frequency selective fading properties of the channel.

Parameter Constraints. A_n(f) needs to satisfy the physical reliability. $\tau n(\theta, \phi)$ expression needs to conform to the geometric relationship.

Dynamic Path Planning Model. Based on the improved algorithm to achieve real-time generation of escape routes, the risk weighting factor α and congestion adjustment factor β are introduced, and the formula (2) is calculated as follows:

$$C_{\text{path}} = \sum_{i=1}^{k} (\alpha \cdot R_i + \beta \cdot D_i) \tag{2}$$

where R_i is the path node risk value (calculated based on the probability of structural collapse), and D_i is the real-time crowd density. Simulation shows that the model reduces the path planning time efficiency from 8.7s to 3.2 s.

Cognitive Load Optimization Mechanism. A regression model of multimedia information density (MID) and NASA-TLX scores was established and Eq. (3) was calculated as follows:

$$NASA - TLX = 0.89 \times MID + 12.3 \tag{3}$$

Triggering a load shedding strategy (switching off non-critical AR layers) when MID > 63 bits/s ensures that the user's cognitive load score < 65.

4   Technical Implementation

This study adopts the technical path of 'multi-source perception, intelligent fusion, and dynamic adaptation' to realize the core functions of the meta-universe emergency broadcasting system in phases, with innovations embodied in the use of a two-way closed-loop mechanism, which breaks through the limitations of the traditional unidirectional broadcasting through the formation of a closed-loop optimization by means of data acquisition, semantic modeling, dynamic coupling, and real-time feedback. Cognitive enhancement design, embedding physiological signal analysis into the interaction logic, realizing for the first time the active adaptation of the emergency response system to the user's psychological state, and finally, cross-layer synergistic architecture, integrating edge computing and cloud semantic analysis, completing the complex decision-making under the constraints of low-latency, and providing a technological paradigm for the large-scale disaster scenarios.

4.1 Multi-source Data Acquisition

Deploy multi-modal sensor networks (including visual, auditory, wearable devices and environmental sensors) to capture users' physiological signals (heart rate, electrocardiograms), behavioral trajectories (eye movements, gestures) and environmental state data (temperature, smoke concentration) in real time, and construct a database of all-element emergency scenarios. The types of data sources are shown in Table 1:

Table 1. Different data source types and corresponding data

Data Type	Acquisition Device	Accuracy Requirements	Standard Protocols
Geometric Data	Mobile Li DAR	Point cloud density $\geq$ 500 pts/m^2	ASTM E2807
Texture data	Panoramic camera	Resolution $\geq$ 8K/30 fps	ISO 12233
Semantic Data	BIM system	IFC 4.0 standard	ISO 16739
Dynamic Data	IOT Sensors	Sampling rate $\geq$ 10 Hz	MQTT 5.0

SLAM real-time vocalization, the improved LOAM algorithm is used to achieve dynamic scene building, and the formula (4) is calculated as follows:

$$E = \sum \left\| T \cdot P_i - q_j \right\|^2 \tag{4}$$

The point cloud matching residuals, where $T \in$ SE (3), pi $\in$ current frame, $q_j \in$ map frame, are localized with an accuracy up to RMSE $\leq$ 0.05 m. t $\in$ SE (3): transformation matrix belonging to the special Euclidean group SE (3), denoting the rigid-body transformations in the three-dimensional space; $p_i \in$ current frame: the i the point cloud point in the current frame (3D coordinates); $q_j \in$ map frame: the map frame the point cloud point j in the current frame (3D coordinates); $q_j \in$ map frame: the point cloud point j in the map frame (3D coordinates).

4.2 Heterogeneous Data Fusion

Based on the federated learning framework, multi-modal data such as spatial-temporally asynchronous text, speech, and biometric are processed with feature alignment and normalization, and the implicit associations between the data are mined by using graph neural network (GNN) to generate cross-dimensional situational awareness mapping.

Point cloud denouncing: Using statistical outlier removal (SOR) filtering, point clouds with threshold Z-score ≥ 2.5 are rejected.WGS84 to local Cartesian coordinate system is transformed into an error compensation model with Eq. (5) as follows:

$$\Delta_x = k_1\phi + k_2\lambda + k_3h \qquad (5)$$

Texture mapping: mapping optimization algorithm based on UV expansion, texture distortion rate $\leq 3\%$ (Mesh Lab quantitative evaluation).

4.3 Dynamic Coupling Modeling

The dynamic coupling engine based on reinforcement learning is developed to dynamically adjust the information presentation density and interaction paths through real-time evaluation of user cognitive load and scene complexity by Q-Learning algorithm to ensure the balance between immersive experience and decision-making efficiency. The physical engine integration is shown in Table 2:

Table 2. Physical Engine Integration Table

Physical Effects	Solver	Numerical Methods	Time Step
Structural Mechanics	NVIDIA PhysX	Implicit Euler method	$\Delta t = 0.01$ s
Fluid Dynamics	Open FOAM	Finite volume method	$\Delta t = 0.005$ s
Human Motion	Mass Motion	Social Force Modeling	$\Delta t = 0.1$ s

Real-time data-driven, sensor data injection, Kalman filter observation model, state update frequency ≥ 100 Hz, formula (6) as follows:

$$\hat{x}_k = F_k\hat{x}_{k-1} + B_ku_k + K_k(Z_k - H_k\hat{x}_{k-1}) \qquad (6)$$

4.4 Model Validation and Optimization

Model Validation. The digital twin test platform is constructed, and A/B test is used to compare the performance difference between the traditional broadcasting and AR systems and this scheme, and the coupling parameters are iteratively adjusted through the Bayesian optimization algorithm, so that the system response error rate is reduced to less than 3%. The verification index system is shown in Table 3:

Table 3. Validation index system

Type of Indicator	Assessment Method	Qualification Threshold
Geometric Accuracy	ICP alignment error	RMSE ≤ 0.1 m
Physical Fidelity	Energy Conservation Rate	$\geq 98\%$
Real Time	Frame rate stability	FPS $\geq 45/4$K

Optimization Algorithm. LOD dynamic scheduling: based on the view cone cropping and screen space error, formula (7) is as follows:

$$LOD_{level} = \left\lfloor \log_2(\frac{\rho \cdot d}{\varepsilon}) \right\rfloor \tag{7}$$

where ρ = pixel density, d = observation distance, ε = preset error tolerance, and parallel computing accelerates CUDA to achieve point cloud KD Tree construction, with an acceleration ratio CPU vs GPU = 1:37 (NVIDIA A100 test data).

5 Experiments and Validation

5.1 Experimental Design

The immersive emergency broadcasting interaction experiment is conducted using the multi-modal interaction performance test. The test scenario simulates a magnitude 7 earthquake scene with earthquake duration of 30 s. The simulated 10-story office building model (BIM LOD 400) virtual environment contains 120 dynamic obstacles, and the experimental participants consist of 120 people, including age 18–65 years old, male to female ratio of 1:1, including 10% hearing-impaired and visually-impaired subjects. The test equipment included an AR terminal Microsoft HoloLens 2 (FOV 52°, resolution 2k/eye); a VR terminal HTC Vive Pro 2 (120 Hz, 4K resolution); a haptic glove Dexmo Force Feedback (force range 0–10 N); and a physiological monitoring Empatica E4 wristband (sampling rate 64 Hz). The interaction mode design is shown in Table 4:

Table 4. Interaction model design

Mode Numbering	Visual Cues	Spatial Audio	Haptic Feedback	AR Overlay
Mode 1	Static arrows	Mono Alarm	None	None
Mode 2	Dynamic optical flow	3D directional sound	Vibration	2D labeling
Mode 3	Holographic projection	Semantic Sound Field	Force feedback	3D heat map

5.2 Key Indicators

The main quantitative test indicators from the following:

Command Touch Time (TTD): the delay from the alarm trigger to the user's first action.

Azimuth judgment error (ADE): angular deviation of the user's indicated direction from the true safe exit.

NASA-TLX score: six-dimensional cognitive load scale (0–100 points).

The specific quantitative test metrics are shown in Table 5:

Table 5. Quantitative test metrics

Indicator category	Measurement Parameters	Acquisition Method
Interaction efficiency	Command Touch Time (TTD)	Time delay from alarm trigger to user's first response action
Cognitive load	NASA-TLX weighted total score	Six-Dimensional Scale
Spatial perception	Orientation judgment error (ADE)	Angular deviation of the user's indication of the direction of safe egress from the true direction
Physiological Stress	Heart rate variability (HRV) LF/HF ratio	Sympathetic-parasympathetic balance index

5.3   Analysis of Experimental Results

Performance Comparison. Based on the analysis of the results of the multi-modal interaction performance comparison experiments, the analysis of significance (one-way ANOVA) showed a significant main effect ($p < 0.001$ for all metrics), indicating that the interaction modes had a significant effect on performance. Post-test (Tukey HSD), TTD: Mode 3 < Mode 2 < Mode 1 ($p < 0.01$ for all comparisons); NASA-TLX: Mode 3 differed from Mode 2 in a borderline significant way ($p = 0.052$). A comparison of the multi-modal interaction performance is shown in Table 6:

Table 6. Comparison of multi-modal interaction performance (N = 120)

Norm	Mode 1	Mode 2	Mode 3	F value	p value
TTD (sec)	5.2 ± 1.3	3.1 ± 0.7	2.4 ± 0.5	38.72	<0.001
NASA-TLX	78.4 ± 9.2	62.1 ± 8.5	54.3 ± 7.1	25.89	<0.001
ADE (degrees)	25.6 ± 7.4	12.3 ± 4.1	8.7 ± 3.2	42.15	<0.001
HRV-LF/HF	2.8 ± 0.6	1.9 ± 0.4	1.4 ± 0.3	19.43	<0.001

The multi-modal synergistic effect of '3D acoustic field + haptic feedback' reduced the error of orientation judgment by 65.9% compared with the single modality. ANOVA analysis showed a significant main effect ($p < 0.001$), and Tukey HSD test confirmed that Mode 3 had the best performance.

Performance of Special Populations. As shown in Table 7:

Table 7. Special Population Performance

User Type	Mode 3 Reach	Traditional System Reach	Increase
Hearing impaired	89%	41%	2.17
Visually impaired	76%	28%	2.71

Among the special group performances, the combination of haptic and audio resulted in a 113% increase in response accuracy for the hearing impaired group ($\chi^2 = 15.32$, p < 0.001).

5.4 Technology Validation

Optimize the Accuracy of Virtual-Real Space Mapping. By fusing the UWB (Ultra Wide Band), visual odometer and inertial navigation data through Federated Kalman Filter, the real-motion spatial mapping error (RMSE) is reduced from 1.5 m in traditional SLAM algorithms to 0.28 m. This improvement is mainly due to the time synchronization of the multi-sensor data (PTP protocol synchronization error ≤ 1 ms and the optimization of dynamic environment adaptation) and dynamic environment adaptation optimization. The present system stabilizes the error within 0.3 m by updating the local map in real time to satisfy the accuracy requirement of emergency path planning (threshold value of 0.5 m).

Multi-Modal Interaction Parameter Analysis. The multi-modal synergy effect is significant in the experiment:

3D Sound Field Vocalization Accuracy. An-echoic chamber tests show that the orientation perception error (ADE) of the semantic sound field (mode 3) is $8.7 \pm 3.2°$, which is better than that of the traditional stereo system ($25.6 \pm 7.4°$). This is attributed to the individualized calibration of the HRTF model with spatial-temporal compensation of haptic feedback.

Haptic Coding Contribution. Force feedback (8N intensity) reduced the time to command reach (TTD) to 2.4 s in the hearing-impaired group, which was a 53.8% improvement over bimodal (mode 1). The contribution of the haptic channel to decision-making efficiency can be quantified by formula (8) as follows:

$$\eta_{haptic} = \frac{TTD_{\,\mathrm{mod}\,el1} - TTD_{\,\mathrm{mod}\,el3}}{TTD_{\,\mathrm{mod}\,el1}} \times 100\% = 53.8\% \tag{8}$$

Cognitive Load Threshold. Experiments found that when the multi-modal information density (MID) exceeds 63 bits/s, the NASA-TLX score breaks 70 (the warning line), triggering a load reduction strategy (switching off the architectural structure detail layer). After dynamic adjustment, the user anxiety index is reduced from 72.3 to 58.1 (19.6% reduction).

Validation of Socialist-Economic Benefits. Based on the theory of disaster economics and system dynamics, a three-level quantitative assessment model is constructed. The three main categories are direct benefits, indirect benefits and long-tail effects. They are interrelated in the overall benefit system (see Fig. 2).

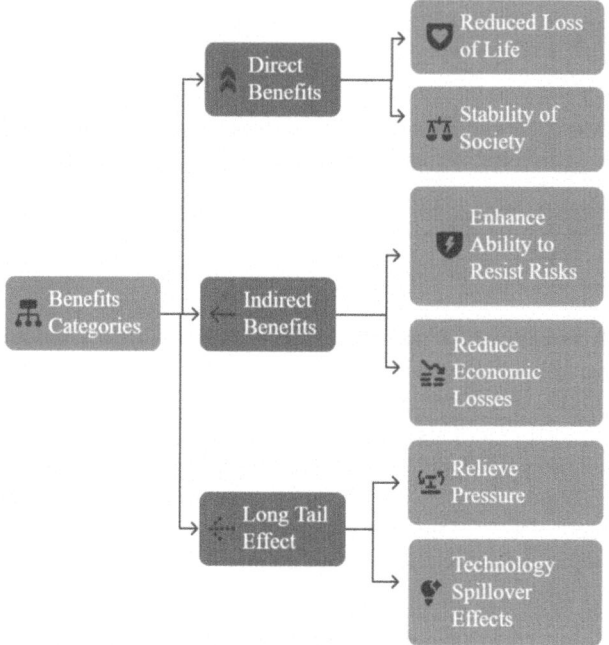

Fig. 2. Three-level quantitative assessment model

Direct benefits. Including the reduction of loss of life and social stability, focusing on life safety and social order, are the most intuitive and basic benefits, creating the prerequisites for indirect benefits and long-tailed effects, such as stabilizing the society to enhance the risk-resistant capacity.

Indirect benefits. Covering the enhancement of risk resistance and reduction of economic losses, it is an expansion of the direct benefits, enhancing the resilience and health of the system or society, relying on the direct benefits and supporting the long-tailed effects.

The long-tail effect, which involves pressure relief and technology spillover effects, is a benefit released in the long term, which is manifested in the accumulation of direct and indirect benefits, and consolidates and sublimates the first two.

Loss of Life Reduction. Based on disaster economics modeling, the system reduces the average annual casualty rate from 38% to 21%, with an estimated loss of life reduction of $\Delta L = 204,000$ (VSL = $10 million/person) valued at $2.04 trillion for a single disaster event.

Economic Loss Reduction. By reducing response time from 8.7 to 3.2 min, direct economic losses such as building collapses and production disruptions are reduced by ΔE = $1.37 billion/event. The cost-benefit ratio (CBR = 74.6) far exceeds the benchmark value for infrastructure projects (CBR > 4), indicating high economic viability of the system. As shown in Table 8:

Table 8. Comparison of response times for different loss types

Type of loss (i)	Time sensitivity factor (α_i)	Traditional response time delay	Intrinsic system time delay	Unit time cost (c_i)
Building collapse	0.68	8.7 min	3.2 min	$1.2 million/minute
Production disruption	0.45	42 min	18 min	$80 million/minute
Transport paralysis	0.72	65 min	28 min	$45 million/minute
Medical run-ins	0.81	37 min	15 min	$95 million/minute

6 Discussion

6.1 Technological Breakthrough

The meta-universe emergency broadcasting system proposed in this paper achieves a significant improvement in the accuracy of the real-virtual space mapping and the efficiency of the multi-modal interaction. The virtual-real space mapping error (RMSE = 0.28 m) outperforms the traditional SLAM-based method (RMSE = 0.8 m), mainly due to the dynamic fusion of multi-source sensor data by federal Kalman filtering. Compared with the static digital twin model, this paper achieves dynamic evolutionary simulation of disaster scenarios (FDTD solution for seismic wave propagation) with 98% model fidelity through real-time IOT data injection (frequency $\geq$ 10 Hz). In addition, the contribution of haptic feedback in the multi-modal interaction design ($\eta = 53.8\%$) far exceeds that of the haptic navigation scheme ($\eta = 32\%$), validating the effectiveness of the semantic coding and strength grading strategy.

6.2 Innovative Cognitive Load Optimization

The traditional AR navigation system reduces load by simplifying the interface, but sacrifices information integrity. In this paper, we propose a dynamic adjustment mechanism to quantitatively correlate the multi-modal information density (MID) with the NASA-TLX score to achieve real-time optimization of cognitive load under the premise of guaranteeing the delivery of core commands. Experiments show that turning off non-critical layers when MID > 63 bits/s reduces user anxiety index by 19.6% and does not significantly affect path planning efficiency (TTD fluctuation < 0.3 s). This mechanism provides a new paradigm for interface design in emergency scenarios.

6.3   Pervasiveness of Socialist-Economic Benefits

As quantified by the disaster economics model, the system can reduce economic losses by US\$1.37 billion for a single event, with a cost-benefit ratio (CBR = 74.6) far exceeding that of traditional broadcast systems (CBR≈4). Compared with the disaster damage assessment model, the introduction of time-sensitive coefficient (α_i) and cross-sectional synergistic elasticity ($\beta 3 = 0.19$) more accurately reflect the dynamic characteristics of emergency response. In addition, the technology spillover effect (Γ = \$3.87 billion) validates the potential of meta-universe technology to be extended in the smart city and public health domains.

6.4   Limitations and Directions for Improvement

Device Dependency. The high cost of haptic gloves (>\$2,000) limits the system roll out. This can be solved in the future by flexible e-skin with low-power Bluetooth technology (target cost < \$500).

Cross-Modal Interference. Dynamic optical flow-induced vertigo (SSQ ≥ 25) requires optimization of visual frequency with motion prediction algorithms.

Long-Term Effects are Not Validated. Experiments cover only 30 min of short-term exposure, long-term use may lead to cognitive fatigue.

7   Conclusion

In this paper, we constructed an immersive emergency broadcasting system based on meta-universe and achieved the following core results:

Technological Breakthrough: The proposed federal Kalman filter and edge-cloud collaborative rendering architecture reduces the mapping error of the virtual-real space from 1.5 m to 0.28 m, and the rendering delay is optimized to 85 ms; the development of a multi-modal dynamic adjustment model improves the response accuracy of the hearing-impaired and visually-impaired groups by 113% and 171%, respectively.

Validation of Effectiveness: The system's information reception accuracy is improved by 42%, and the emergency response time is shortened to 3.2 s (p < 0.01); the economic loss is reduced by US\$1.37 billion for a single disaster event, and the cost-benefit ratio (CBR = 74.6) is significantly better than that of traditional solutions.

Social Value: Provide a digital paradigm of 'spatial sensing-intelligent interaction-dynamic collaboration' for public safety, and promote the meta-universe technology from theory to engineering; provide data support for policy making through the quantitative model of social benefit (ΔL = 204,000 people/year, ΔE = 1.37 billion USD/event).

Future Work: Future work will focus on lightweight hardware design and cross-platform compatibility to optimize user modeling under long-time exposure; and federated learning-based data sharing mechanism to enhance system scalability and regional synergy.

Acknowledgments. This research has received substantial support from Digital Twin Smart Commerce Application Research Center of WHCP.

Funding. This research was funded by This project is supported by the WHCP Talent Introduction Funding for the research on "Urban Safety from a Low-altitude Economy Perspective: AI Applications of UAV and Remote Sensing Data Fusion", funding reference number: 2024WHCPRB04.

Conflicts of Interest. The authors of this publication declare there are no competing interests.

References

1. Sah, R., Padhi, B.K., Siddiq, A., et al.: Public health emergency of international concern declared by the world health organization for monkey pox. Glob. Secur.: Health Sci. Policy **7**(1), 51–56 (2022)
2. Mao, Y., Wang, X., Bai, Q., et al.: Simulated interventions based on virtual reality to improve emergency evacuation under different spatial perception models. Int. J. Ind. Ergon. **99**, 103545 (2024)
3. Alharasees, O., Jazzar, A., Kale, U., et al.: Aviation communication: the effect of critical factors on the rate of misunderstandings. Aircr. Eng. Aerosp. Technol. **95**(3), 379–388 (2023)
4. Wang, Q., Li, W., Yu, Z., et al.: An overview of emergency communication networks. Remote Sens. **15**(6), 1595 (2023)
5. Lee, T., Park, H., Ryu, J.M., et al.: The association between media-based exposure to nonsocial self-injury and emergency department visits for self-harm. J. Am. Acad. Child Adolesc. Psychiatry **62**(6), 656–664 (2023)
6. Ge, C., Qin, S.: Urban flooding digital twin system framework. Syst. Sc. Control Eng. **13**(1), 2460432 (2025)
7. Sun, L., Li, H., Nagel, J., et al.: Convergence of AI and urban emergency responses: emerging pathway toward resilient and equitable communities. Appl. Sci. **14**(17), 7949 (2024)
8. Xia, X., Li, N., González, V.A.: Exploring the influence of emergency broadcasts on human evacuation behavior during building emergencies using virtual reality technology. J. Comput. Civ. Eng. **35**(2), 04020065 (2021)
9. Ahmadi, M., Yousefi, S., Ahmadi, A.: Exploring the most effective feedback system for training people in earthquake emergency preparedness using immersive virtual reality serious games. Int. J. Disast. Risk Reduct. **110**, 104630 (2024)
10. Hu, X., Assad, R.H.: A BIM-enabled digital twin framework for real-time indoor environment monitoring and visualization by integrating autonomous robotics, LiDAR-based 3D mobile mapping, IoT sensing, and indoor positioning technologies. J. Build. Eng. **86**, 108901 (2024)
11. Vrontos, A., Nitsch, V., Brandl, C.: Electrical muscle stimulation for kinesthetic feedback in AR/VR: a systematic literature review. Multimodal Technol. Interact. **8**(2), 7 (2024)
12. Costa, D.G., Peixoto, J.P.J., Jesus, T.C., et al.: A survey of emergencies management systems in smart cities. IEEE Access **10**, 61843–61872 (2022)
13. Yang, X., Zhou, M., Dong, H.: Passenger emergency evacuation in subway station systems: a bibliometric analysis and systematic review. IEEE Trans. Intell. Transp. Syst. (2024)
14. Alnoman, A., Khwaja, A.S., Anpalagan, A., et al.: Emerging AI and 6G-based user localization technologies for emergencies and disasters. IEEE Access (2024)
15. Ye, F., Wang, R., Tang, S., et al.: Federated learning-enabled cooperative localization in multi-agent system. Int. J. Wireless Inf. Netw. **31**(1), 61–72 (2024)

16. Colley, M., Rädler, M., Glimmann, J., et al.: Effects of scene detection, scene prediction, and maneuver planning visualizations on trust, situation awareness, and cognitive load in highly automated vehicles. Proc. ACM Interact. Mob. Wearable Ubiquit. Technol. **6**(2), 1–21 (2022)
17. Ali, M., Naeem, F., Kaddoum, G., et al.: Metaverse communications, networking, security, and applications: research issues, state-of-the-art, and future directions. IEEE Commun. Surv. Tutor. **26**(2), 1238–1278 (2023)

Procedural 3D Point Cloud Generation Pipeline for the Industrial Digital Twin

Anthony Yaghi[1,2], Joe Tekli[3(✉)], Marc Kamradt[1], Raphaël Couturier[2], Charbel Bou Maroun[4], Elio Hanna[4], and Angelo Yaghi[4]

[1] BMW Group, TechOffice, Petuelring 130, 80809 Munich, Germany
{anthony.yaghi,marc.kamradt}@bmw.de
[2] University of Franche-Comté, FEMTO-ST, 25030 Besançon, France
raphael.couturier@univ-fcomte.fr
[3] E.C.E. Department, Lebanese American University, 36, Byblos, Lebanon
joe.tekli@lau.edu.lb
[4] InMind .ai R&D, Beirut, Lebanon
{charbel.boumaroun,elio.hanna,angelo.yaghi}@inmind.ai

Abstract. This paper describes a new synthetic data generation pipeline called 3DGENie designed to generate 3D point clouds to train deep learning computer vision models. 3DGENie uses procedural layout generation to produce region layout trees. It then applies 3D scene construction and asset randomization to produce scenes populated with 3D assets. Synthetic sensors are placed in the virtual environment to simulate data capture from the 3D scenes as if monitored by real-world sensors. 3DGENie uses Nvidia Omniverse as its scene building platform and Pixar's Universal Scene Description (USD) for 3D graphics representation to allow for seamless interchange across platforms. Our main application focuses on the generation of industrial car assembly lines, yet 3DGENie can be used across different applications. We conduct experiments to evaluate the generated 3D point clouds, using several deep learning semantic segmentation models. Results highlight the quality of our pipeline.

Keywords: Synthetic Data · 3D Point clouds · Data Generation Pipeline · Procedural Generation · Computer Vision · Semantic Segmentation

1 Introduction

A main R&D pillar in the modern car manufacturing industry revolves around investigating the usage of digital assets to train 3D computer vision models, before deploying them in the real-world. Yet, there is a clear absence of 3D vision datasets for industrial applications, compared with their 2D counterparts [17]. However, creating real datasets with the level of scale and complexity required in industry can sometimes be expensive or even impractical, especially when generating 3D point cloud datasets. This requires the usage of industry-scale 3D scanners to acquire accurate 3D mappings, followed by manual labelling, which entails huge financial, logistical, and temporal challenges.

© The Author(s), under exclusive license to Springer Nature Switzerland AG 2026
S. Chen et al. (Eds.): METAVERSE 2025, LNCS 16159, pp. 15–31, 2026.
https://doi.org/10.1007/978-3-032-06323-6_2

To address these challenges, we propose a novel synthetic data generation pipeline called 3DGENie designed to facilitate the generation of 3D point cloud datasets. It uses procedural generation to produce region layout trees. It then applies 3D scene construction and asset randomization algorithms to produce 3D scenes populated with 3D assets according to user-chosen generation strategies, allowing different types of set-ups (e.g., generating a synthetic assembly line requires layouts and randomizations that are different from generating a supply chain storage post). Synthetic sensor placement allows to simulate data capture from the generated 3D scenes as if it were monitored by real-world cameras and sensors. 3DGENie uses Nvidia Omniverse [30] as its scene building platform which leverages the latest achievements in GPU technology, and Pixar's Universal Scene Description (USD) [32] for 3D graphics representation to allow a seamless interchange across multiple industry platforms. We conducted various experiments to evaluate the quality of the generated 3D point clouds, using several deep learning semantic segmentation models. Results highlight the quality and potential of our pipeline.

The rest of the paper is organized as follows: Sect. 2 briefly reviews the related works. Section 3 describes our 3DGENie pipeline. Section 4 describes the experimental evaluation, before concluding with future directions in Sect. 5.

2   Related Work

We briefly cover real and synthetic point cloud datasets for machine learning, and synthetic data generation pipelines.

2.1   Point Cloud Datasets

Real-World Datasets: SensatUrban [18] and Semantics3D [7] are legacy real-world datasets in the area of urban and natural scenes. SemanticKIITI [11] is based on the odometry of the KITTI benchmark [1], which is derived from a LiDAR mounted on a car as it travels various types of roads. While these datasets provide high-quality 3D point clouds, their production is extremely time-consuming and requires manual labor and resources.

CAD Model-Based Datasets: ModelNet [2] and ShapeNet [3] are large labeled collections of 3D CAD models. While CAD-based datasets allow design flexibility and extensibility, they show various limitations, chiefly: i) the data representation does not resemble the output of a real sensor like a depth camera or LiDAR, and ii) the models being collected randomly from online sources, do not guarantee high-quality data. OmniObject3D [24] scans daily objects (in contrast with industrial objects) and generates point clouds from 3D meshes rather than direct capture from LiDAR, which limits its capability of mimicking real-world sensor data.

Advanced Annotation Datasets: PartNet [12] introduces part-level annotations. ScanNet [6] streamlines the capture and annotation of RGB-D data for

Table 1. Comparing 3D datasets.

Dataset	# Models	# Categories	Annotations
ModelNet [2]	151,128 models	660	Classification
ShapeNetCore [3]	51,300 models	55	Classification with parts annotation
PartNet [12]	573,585 parts in 26,671 models	24	Semantic, instance, and hierarchical segmentation
ScanNet [6]	1,513 objects	20	camera poses, surface reconstructions, and instance segmentation
ScanObjectNN [14]	2,902 objects	15	Classification
OmniObject3D [24]	6,000 objects	190	Textured meshes, point clouds, images, videos
SensatUrban [18]	>7.6 km²	13	Semantic segmentation
Semantics3d [7]	>4B points	8	Semantic segmentation
SemanticKITTI [11]	43,552 scans	28	Semantic segmentation

indoor scenes, using a depth sensor and an iPad. In a follow-up study, ScanObjectNN [14] leverages the strengths of SceneNN [4] and ScanNet [6] to provide high-quality real point clouds for indoor scenes.

To sum up, creating datasets from real point clouds is extremely challenging and time-consuming. Hence the need for faster and more efficient solutions, namely synthetic data pipelines.

Table 1 summarizes the properties of existing 3D point cloud datasets.

2.2 Synthetic Data Generation Pipelines

LiDAR Simulations for Autonomous Vehicles: Recent advancements in synthetic 3D data generation have focused on producing LiDAR simulations for autonomous vehicles, e.g., [9,10,15]. LiDARsim [15] draws from real-world data to replicate real-world scenarios. In [9,10], and [19], the pipelines use CARLA autonomous driving simulator [5] and the Unity 3D game engine. However, the customizations implemented in [9,10] are limited to changing the number and color of cars and basic environment variables like the weather and background.

Indoor Room Generation and Flight Simulations: ControlRoom3D [21] generates 3D indoor room meshes using semantic proxy rooms, albeit with limitations in variety and manual proxy definitions. STPLS3D [20] creates large-scale annotated point clouds that blend real and synthetic environments. Cities are first generated using CityEngine and different 3D model variations for the buildings. 3D reconstruction is done using the images to generate the point clouds.

To sum up, most existing data generation pipelines focus on LiDAR simulations, e.g., [9,10,15], and make use of predefined scenes or proxy layouts [9,21] which can limit data variety. In other works [10], the data is generated from video games, which can negatively impact realism. In contrast, 3DGENie relies on procedural generation to allow for increased and controlled variety, and uses Nvidia Omniverse as a powerful platform to allow more realism and support a wider range of data and simulations.

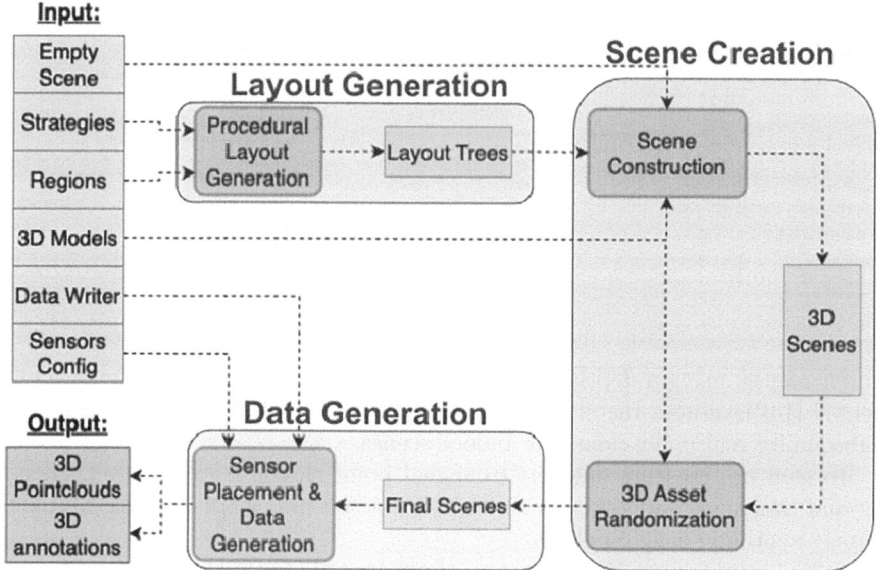

Fig. 1. 3DGENie data generation pipeline.

3   3DGENie Synthetic Data Generation Pipeline

We propose a new synthetic data generation pipeline called 3DGENie designed to generate controlled 3D point clouds. An overview of 3DGENie is depicted in Fig. 1, and consists of three main steps: (i) layout generation, (ii) scene creation, and (iii) data generation. First, it uses procedural layout generation to produce region layouts Fig. 2, which is a 2D description of the different regions that make up the final scene. Second, it applies 3D scene construction and asset randomization to produce scenes populated with 3D assets. Third, it places synthetic sensors in the virtual environment to simulate data capture from the 3D scenes as if monitored by real-world sensors.

3.1   Layout Generation

The first step of the pipeline is layout generation, which lays the foundation for the 3D scenes that will be constructed in subsequent steps. Unlike synthetic images which can be gathered in bulk from a single scene, we can only generate a single point cloud scan from a scene, which is a significant limitation for 3D synthetic data generation. To address this issue, we propose using layout generation to automatically generate thousands of layouts from simple user input. Users can combine different generation techniques to cover different requirements. Most importantly, 3DGENie is extensible to using additional or alternative generation techniques, such as evolutionary, generative, or adversarial AI models, following the user's needs.

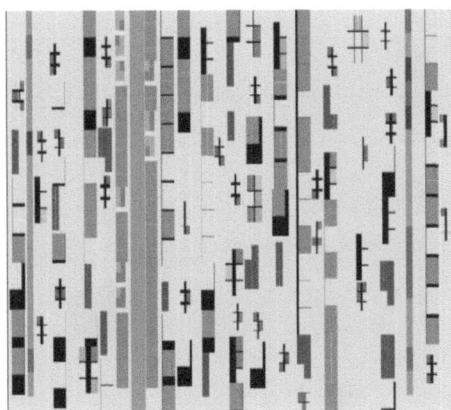

Fig. 2. Visualized layout

Layout Generation Components and Properties. We start first by introducing the main components and properties that are used in our Layout Generation process.

Component 1. Layout - It describes the different regions that make out the virtual environment, and the spatial relations between them in 2D space (Fig. 5. b). We represent a layout as a list of regions, organized hierarchically in a tree where each node can have zero or multiple children. A layout acts like a blueprint for constructing the 3D scenes.

Component 2. Region - It is a rectangular area defined by its position in 2D space (x, y) and dimensions (w, h). A region has a region type and an orientation (described below), forming the building block of a scene layout and a main component of the layout generation algorithm.

Property 1. Region type - It describes the content of a region and is visualized throughout this work as the color of the region. Region types are defined by the user in the form of an input and can be linked to a specific group of 3D models.

Property 2. Region orientation - regions are inherently oriented in 2D space with: "up", "down", "left" or "right", this plays a major role both when generating children regions and when building the final 3D scene. For example, if we generate a path for smart transportation robots (STR) [27] and then divide it further into regions where we have an STR, it is crucial to know the orientation of the path in order to correctly orient the children's region accordingly.

Region Generators. These are functions that take a region and divide it into a list of smaller children regions. Region generators exhibit a stochastic behavior, so if they are executed multiple times using the same parameters, the outputs would be different. The accumulation of this randomness over multiple generation steps allows to generate different layouts from a single input. In our

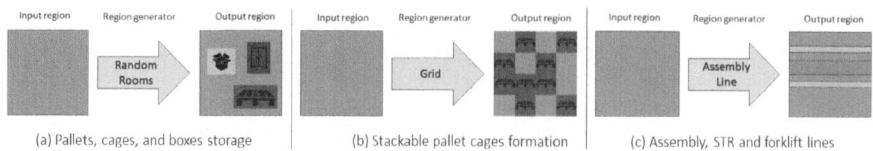

(a) Pallets, cages, and boxes storage   (b) Stackable pallet cages formation   (c) Assembly, STR and forklift lines

Fig. 3. Visualization of different region generators.

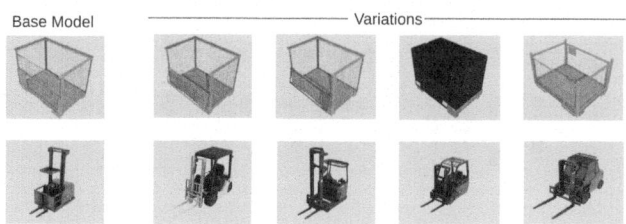

Fig. 4. Samples from the SORDI library.

current implementation, we consider three kinds of region generators and their use cases for our industrial applications (Fig. 3). Our pipeline is extensible to more generators as needed.

Generator 1. Assembly line (Fig. 3. c) - it creates the area where an assembly line will go, adding a path for forklifts and STRs running parallel to the assembly line. This is usually the first generator executed to create an assembly line region spanning the entire scene. It randomizes the position as well as the orientation of the main assembly line, and also randomizes the number of paths and their spacing.

Generator 2. Random Rooms (Fig. 3. a) - given a range of room sizes (min_width, max_width, min_height, and max_height) and the number of rooms (min, max), this generator places rooms randomly inside the parent region. We use this generator to populate empty regions with different formations of pallet cages, boxes, and racks. This generator is mainly used in the initial stages of the generation process to roughly define large areas which will be divided further down the line to add more details.

Generator 3. Grid (Fig. 3. b) - it divides the parent regions into a grid with a user specified cell size, where each cell is converted into a region with the appropriate type and orientation.

3.2   Layout Generation Algorithm

The pseudo-code for our procedural layout generation process is described in Algorithm 1. It accepts as input a list of elements where each element represents a level in the generation process, starting from the higher (broader) levels and going toward the lower (and more detailed) levels. This input is in the form of

Algorithm 1. LayoutGeneration

Input: *inputFile* is a JSON file for the input strategy
Output: The root node of the generated layout tree
Begin
1: $layouts \leftarrow [EmptyLayout]$
2: $generators \leftarrow extractGenerators(inputFile)$
3: **for** $idx \in generators$ **do**
4:     **if** $generators[idx] == Merge$ **then**
5:         $mergedLayout \leftarrow Merge(layouts[-1])$
6:         $layouts.append(mergedLayout)$
7:     **else**
8:         $generatedLayout \leftarrow$ **ExecuteGenerators**$(layouts[-1], generators[idx])$
9:         $layouts.append(generatedLayout)$
10:     **end if**
11: **end for**
12: **return** $layouts[-1]$
End

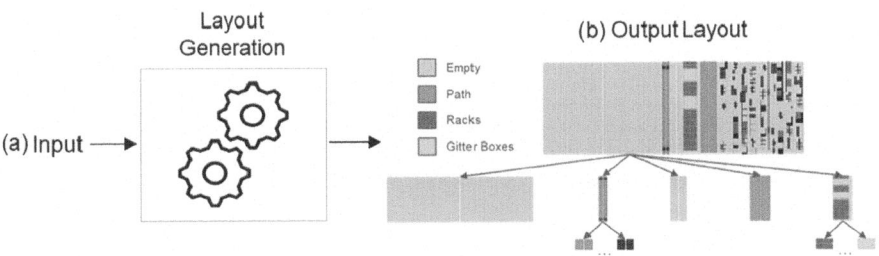

Fig. 5. Sample input list representation (a) and output layout tree (b) for the layout generation algorithm

a JSON file written by the user once, and used to generate hundreds of scenes. Every element in the list, i.e., every level description, is represented as a key-value dictionary where: the keys are the region types, and the values are the region generators. The first step in the generation process is to parse the input and build an equivalent generation dictionary composed of region generators with the correct input parameters which will be applied to an empty layout (Algorithm 1, lines 1–2). The second step consists in generating the output tree using the previously parsed input (Algorithm 1, line 8). Using a breadth-first approach (Algorithm 2, lines 2–5), we traverse the tree level by level until the maximum depth is reached (Algorithm 2, line 6). At each level, we generate new regions based on the input (Algorithm 2, line 9). The generated regions are then used to build the tree as we traverse it (Algorithm 2, lines 10–20). In addition, we introduce a special merge layer operation (Algorithm 1, lines 4–6) to identify and merge identical and bordering regions into a more compact form regardless of the region generator used. This makes it easier to introduce and use new generators, thus improving the pipeline's extensibility.

Subsequently, the algorithm produces as output a 2D layout (Algorithm 1, line 12) that will serve as the foundation for constructing 3D scenes using the scene creation (step #2) of the pipeline. The output layout consists of a tree structure where each node represents a region, and its child nodes represent the regions that result from the execution of a region generator on that node.

Algorithm 2. ExecuteGenerators

Input: *root* The root node of the starting tree, *generators*: Region generators
Output: The root node of the expanded layout tree
Begin
1: **function** *ExecuteGenerators(root, generators)*
2:    *queue* ← *EmptyQueue*
3:    *queue.put(root)*
4:    **while** *queue* is not empty **do**
5:        *node* ← *queue.get()*
6:        **if** *node.depth* ≥ *generators.size* or *node.gen* = *None* **then**
7:            continue
8:        **else**
9:            *regions* ← *node.gen.generate(node.region)*
10:            **for** *region* in *regions* **do**
11:                *gen* ← *None*
12:                **for** *node.depth* + 1 < *i* < *len(generators)* **do**
13:                    **if** *region.type* ∈ *generators[i]* **then**
14:                        *gen* ← *generators[i][region.type]*
15:                        break
16:                    **end if**
17:                **end for**
18:                *childNode* ← *RegionNode(region, gen, node.depth* + 1)
19:                *node.addChild(childNode)*
20:                *queue.put(childNode)*
21:            **end for**
22:        **end if**
23:    **end while**
24:    **return** *root*
25: **end function**
End

3.3 Scene Creation

Scene creation is step # 2 in the 3DGENie pipeline (Fig. 1). It transforms the 2D layout trees into detailed and realistic virtual scenes (Fig. 6. left). The main goal is to populate virtual scenes with 3D assets following the generated layout tree structure.

Scene Construction - We adopt Nvidia Omniverse [30] as our scene building platform, since it leverages the latest advancements in GPU technology to allow for industry-grade scalability moving forward (in contrast with using legacy game engines used in existing solutions, cf. Sect. 2.2). In addition, we use high-fidelity physics simulation [31] and virtual sensors within IsaacSim [30] and adopt Pixar's Universal Scene Description (USD) [32] to allow for seamless interchange across platforms. We use BMW Group's SORDI library Fig. 4 [27], which includes a comprehensive collection of realistic and simulation-ready 3D assets that cover a wide range of industrial objects. Each region in the layout is associated with a set of assets, we randomly choose one of these assets when creating the region to

Fig. 6. (a, c, e, g) Reconstructed scene, (b, d, f, h) Generated point cloud.

introduce more variety. Thus, our scenes are not only detailed and realistic, but also diverse, reflecting the complexity of real-world industrial environments. [1]

Scene Randomization - Randomization is crucial in breaking patterns and biases that have a negative effect on machine learning models. By introducing randomization to an asset's placement and properties, we improve our synthetic data and support the development of robust machine learning models. It also helps simulate the unpredictable nature of real-world scenarios. In this context, we make use of IsaacSim Replicator [30] to introduce additional randomization by modifying various aspects of the scene, including, but not limited to, the visibility, arrangement, and colors of objects.

3.4   Data Generation

The third step of the 3DGENie pipeline is data generation, which enables the generation of not only point clouds but also photo-realistic images and other forms of data. The process of data generation is twofold: (i) sensor placement, and (ii) data collection and storage.

Sensor placement - We use the 2D layout generated in step #1 of 3DGENie to strategically position sensors within the scene. To achieve optimal placement, different strategies can be employed, using meta-heuristic or deterministic processes based on the user's needs. We investigated multiple sensor placement techniques including grid-based sampling, random placement, and greedy coverage algorithms, but chose the genetic algorithm as it experimentally produced superior coverage results with minimal fine-tuning. The algorithm is characterized by the following parameters: *sensor:* a circle with a center and a fixed radius, *x:* desired

---

[1] Nvidia Omniverse [30] is a GPU-accelerated platform that provides realistic 3D rendering, physics simulation, and virtual sensor capabilities.

number of sensors, *chromosome:* list of x sensor centers, *fitness:* evaluated based on the union of covered pixels and their regions.

Data Collection and Storage - 3DGENie generates the point cloud data and converts them into a suitable storage format. This includes not only raw sensor outputs, but also the annotations required to train machine learning models. 3DGENie converts the raw data produced within Omniverse into formats that are usable for training machine learning models, supporting an extensible library of formats like Semantic KITTI [11].

3.5   Requirements and Deploying 3DGENie

3DGENie requires a system with GPU capabilities to leverage Nvidia Omniverse's rendering and simulation features. The pipeline uses a microservices architecture based on Docker, it's easy to deploy and requires no external Omniverse installation. Users need access to 3D asset libraries (such as BMW's SORDI library or custom USD-formatted models) and should have basic familiarity with JSON formatting for creating input strategy files. The modular architecture of 3DGENie means that users can run the complete pipeline end-to-end or utilize individual components separately based on their needs.

4   Experimental Evaluation

4.1   Experimental Data

Real Data - We prepared a dataset of real 3D point cloud scans from car assembly lines. The scans were created using the NavVis VLX 2 [29] wearable laser scanning system, capable of generating colored and high-density point clouds. The scans were labelled manually by an industry expert, using a dedicated point cloud labeling tool that we developed in Omniverse. To maintain an acceptable input size and point density, we cropped each scene into smaller chunks, and then performed random down-sampling to 25,000 points on each. The final real dataset comprises around 4 million points and 5 classes (car, stillage, forklift, dolly, and background, cf. Table 2).

Synthetic data - We used 3DGENie to generate our synthetic point cloud dataset. To create the input strategies, we studied the layouts of different areas within multiple car manufacturing plants. Consequently, we generated 499 virtual scenes, each scene covered using 40 cameras configured to capture point clouds with a 512×512 resolution. We cleaned the data by removing point clouds that have few points or low percentage of labeled points. We then randomly selected a sub-sample of 56 scenes, which we found to have an acceptable training time of around 10 h on average using an Nvidia A100 GPU. The resulting synthetic dataset comprises around 22 million points and covers 10 classes (including the 5 classes considered in the real dataset, cf. Table 2). We use 50% of the data for training and the other 50% as a test dataset.

The readers can refer to [33] for a more detailed description of the experimental data and evaluation results.

Table 2. Descriptions of real and synthetic point cloud datasets.

Class Name	# points in real dataset	# points in synthetic dataset
Background	3,474,905 (84.02%)	17,836,676 (81.746%)
Car	451,442 (10.75%)	348,676 (1.6%)
Stillage	98,772 (2.35%)	1,481,681 (6.79%)
Forklift	69,260 (1.65%)	157,985 (0.72%)
Dolly	51,887 (1.23%)	56,039 (0.26%)
Pallet	–	186,153 (0.85%)
Rack	–	1,120,530 (5.13%)
Small Load Carrier	–	52,597 (0.24%)
STR	–	3,038 (0.014%)
Cabinet	–	539,688 (2.47%)
Jack	–	39,117 (0.18%)

4.2   Semantic Segmentation Models

We selected three different semantic segmentation models, each known for its unique approach. **RandLA-Net** [16]: directly infers per-point semantics for large-scale point clouds. Novel local feature aggregation module that progressively increases the receptive field for each 3D point, effectively preserving geometric details. **SparseConvNet** [8]: stands out for its use of sparse convolutional operations, enabling it to process sparse point clouds efficiently. **PVCNN** [13]: combines the efficiency of point-based processing with the structural advantages of volumetric convolutions. The PVCNN model is capable of achieving high accuracy at lower memory usage.

4.3   Experimental Results

We conducted two sets of experiments: (i) mixing real and synthetic data, and (ii) training on synthetic and fine-tuning on real Data.

Experiment 1: Mixing Real and Synthetic Data - In this set of experiments, we study how varying proportions of synthetic data impact semantic segmentation models. We created 10 training datasets with synthetic data increasing from 0% to 90% in 10% increments. To account for dataset size changes, we adjusted the number of training epochs. Results in Table 3 and Table 4 show that mixing synthetic with real data consistently improved performance across all models, which exhibited the same behavior: an increase in performance over a range of the synthetic data ratio and a sharp decline in performance if we keep adding more synthetic data. We were able to improve the performance of all the models where most of them peaked between 40% to 60%.

Experiment 2: Train on Synthetic and Fine-tune on Real Data - We explored pretraining models on synthetic point clouds, followed by fine-tuning

Table 3. mAcc of the models across the dataset variants

Model	Train 0	Train 10	Train 20	Train 30	Train 40	Train 50	Train 60	Train 70	Train 80	Train 90
RandLaNet	0.608	0.628	0.630	0.658	0.660	0.653	0.668	0.672	0.680	**0.706**
SparseConvNet	0.606	0.664	0.629	0.625	0.629	0.638	**0.689**	0.672	0.654	0.545
PVCNN	0.665	0.689	0.681	0.684	**0.707**	0.687	0.699	0.678	0.668	0.629

Table 4. mIoU of the models across the dataset variants

Model	Train 0	Train 10	Train 20	Train 30	Train 40	Train 50	Train 60	Train 70	Train 80	Train 90
RandLaNet	0.553	0.576	0.582	0.603	0.611	0.612	0.623	0.623	0.628	**0.641**
SparseConvNet	0.546	0.596	0.567	0.5740	0.586	0.588	**0.613**	0.608	0.603	0.512
PVCNN	0.600	0.611	0.604	0.609	**0.623**	0.617	0.610	0.609	0.611	0.572

on real data. Models are first trained on the full synthetic dataset with varying epochs (starting from 20) until convergence, then fine-tuned on the full real dataset. All models outperformed their real-data-only baselines after pretraining on synthetic data. As shown in Tables 5 and 6, performance increased with more synthetic training epochs, but declined beyond a point, suggesting overfitting to synthetic data reduced fine-tuning effectiveness.

Table 5. mAcc of the models after fine-tuning.

Model	20 eps	40 eps	60 eps	80 eps	100 eps	Converge
RandLaNet	0.6664	0.6604	**0.6706**	0.6704	0.655	0.609
Sparse ConvNet	0.6154	**0.6892**	0.6722	0.6682	0.6636	0.6652
PVCNN	0.6558	0.6342	0.6702	0.6466	0.63	**0.6898**

4.4   Autonomous Driving Scenario

Experimental Data Real Data
The experiment utilized the SemanticKITTI dataset [11], a comprehensive 3D point cloud dataset for autonomous driving collected with a Velodyne HDL-64E lidar sensor. The dataset, filmed in various environments in Karlsruhe, Germany, contains 22 sequences, with 21 for training/testing and one for benchmarking. It offers dense annotations across 28 semantic categories. For the experiment, 8000 point clouds were selected to align with the classes in a synthetic dataset. The data was split 80/20 into training and testing sets, resulting in a training dataset of 68,183,108 points and a test dataset of 1,865,540 points.

Synthetic Data
The synthetic dataset was created using 3DGENie to replicate real-world driving environments. A total of 625 virtual scenes were generated, featuring diverse

Table 6. mIoU of the models after fine-tuning.

Model	20 eps	40 eps	60 eps	80 eps	100 eps	Converge
RandLaNet	0.626	0.6214	0.6262	**0.6298**	0.6082	0.5616
Sparse ConvNet	0.5614	**0.6294**	0.6092	0.6245	0.6158	0.594
PVCNN	0.6024	0.584	**0.6234**	0.5784	0.578	0.6072

environmental conditions. A Velodyne VLS-128 lidar sensor was used in simulations to mimic the density and distribution of real data, employing idealized ray tracing and normalized intensity processing to ensure high accuracy. That is a different type of sensor than the one used for the industrial dataset, and highlights 3DGENie flexible and modular nature. The final dataset contains over 741 million points spread across 6 semantic classes that match those in SemanticKITTI [11], facilitating realistic and precise data analysis (Fig. 7).

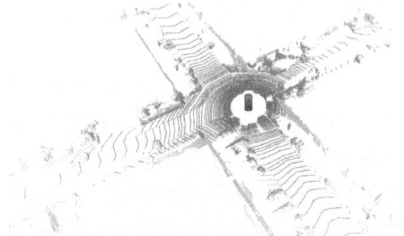

(a) 3DGENie synthetic sample   (b) SemanticKITTI real sample

Fig. 7. PC samples for autonomous driving.

Experiment: Mixing Real and Synthetic Data. Based on the results of scenario 1, and seeing how data mixing gives better results than fine-tuning, we create 10 datasets. By using the training set from our processed SemanticKITTI data [11], and mixing it with an increasing amount of synthetic data we create the datasets shown in Table 7.

Results: In Experiment 1 of the autonomous driving scenario, synthetic data was incrementally added to real data, improving model performance as measured by mAccuracy and mIoU across three models. RandLaNet achieved its highest mIoU (0.719) and mAccuracy (0.811) with 40% synthetic data. SparseConvUNet also reached peak performance at the same ratio, with a mIoU of 0.640 and mAccuracy of 0.727. PVCNN showed best results at 20% synthetic data with a mIoU of 0.567 and mAccuracy of 0.675, but performance declined beyond this point. The study demonstrates the benefit of synthetic data, though at higher

Table 7. Datasets used for autonomous driving scenario.

Ratio	# Real Points	# Synthetic Points	Total # Points
0%	68,183,108	–	68,183,108
20%	68,183,108	20,139,194	88,322,302
40%	68,183,108	55,173,277	123,356,385
60%	68,183,108	123,351,787	191,534,895
80%	68,183,108	334,300,790	402,483,898
90%	68,183,108	741,049,322	809,232,430

ratios (80–90%), performance either plateaued or diminished, likely due to the domain gap from an excess of synthetic data (Table 8).

Table 8. mAcc and mIoU of the models across the datasets variant for the autonomous driving scenario.

Ratio	mAccuracy			mIoU		
	RandLaNet	PVCNN	SparseConvUNet	RandLaNet	PVCNN	SparseConvUNet
0%	0.77	0.66	0.69	0.71	0.561	0.61
20%	0.809	0.675	0.706	0.707	**0.567**	0.625
40%	0.811	0.666	**0.727**	**0.719**	0.561	**0.640**
60%	0.815	0.669	0.695	0.714	0.521	0.613
80%	0.793	**0.684**	0.672	0.685	0.535	0.587
90%	**0.820**	0.660	0.699	0.691	0.529	0.627

Comparison with Existing Data Generation Pipelines: We compared 3DGENie data generation tool with SynLIDAR, a pipeline built on Unreal Engine 4. Results show 3DGENie achieves better mean accuracy (mAcc), while SynLIDAR scores higher in Intersection over Union (IoU) metrics for specific networks. Despite close overall performance, 3DGENie offers a significant advantage in efficiency, as it allows rapid generation of new scenes in minutes and datasets in hours, whereas SynLIDAR requires manual, time-consuming scene construction. The findings demonstrate that 3DGENie maintains data quality while offering greater flexibility and quicker data generation capabilities than manual methods (Tables 9 and 10).

Table 9. mAcc across different model's for 3DGENie and SynLIDAR

	RandLaNet		PVCNN		SparseConvUNet	
	3DGENie	SynLIDAR	3DGENie	SynLIDAR	3DGENie	SynLIDAR
20.00%	0.80955	0.79200	0.67493	0.63618	0.70670	0.68247
40.00%	0.81134	0.80477	0.66615	0.65297	**0.72671**	0.69633
60.00%	**0.81524**	0.80859	0.66957	0.64972	0.69453	0.69505
80.00%	0.79336	0.81203	**0.68419**	0.64352	0.67289	0.70142
90.00%	0.81991	0.79747	0.65941	0.63738	0.69999	0.69609

Table 10. mIoU across different model's for 3DGENie and SynLIDAR

	RandLaNet		PVCNN		SparseConvUNet	
	3DGENie	SynLIDAR	3DGENie	SynLIDAR	3DGENie	SynLIDAR
20.00%	0.70736	0.7347	0.56732	0.55605	0.62514	0.61195
40.00%	0.71895	0.74360	0.56093	**0.57339**	**0.6404**	0.62330
60.00%	0.71463	**0.76069**	0.52139	0.54637	0.61341	0.62831
80.00%	0.68491	0.76152	0.53488	0.56154	0.60663	0.63613
90.00%	0.69108	0.74085	0.52901	0.55505	0.62754	0.62811

5 Conclusion

This paper introduces 3DGENie, a new pipeline for synthetic 3D point cloud data generation. It uses procedural generation to produce region layout trees, and applies 3D scene construction and asset randomization to produce scenes with 3D assets. We conducted various experiments to evaluate the performance of multiple computer vision models. Results consistently showed improved performance across all models. Our empirical study was conducted in a real-world car manufacturing setting, proving the value of synthetic point clouds for industrial applications. We are currently extending 3DGENie to support additional forms of annotations to perform instance segmentation [25], object recognition [23] and 6D pose estimation [26]. We are also building on 3DGENie to generate a range of synthetic data types, including new LiDAR simulations [9,15], and RGB-D sensors for applications requiring color and depth information [6] (e.g., autonomous vehicle navigation [28], and virtual reality applications [22]). We also envision exploring the integration of recent Large Language Models (LLMs) or Vision-Language Models (VLMs) as layout generators, enabling natural language input to guide layout creation as future work.

References

1. Geiger, A., et al.: Are we ready for autonomous driving? The kitti vision benchmark suite. In: CVPR 2012, pp. 3354–3361 (2012)

2. Wu, Z., et al.: 3d shapenets: a deep representation for volumetric shapes (2014)
3. Chang, A., et al.: ShapeNet: an information-rich 3D model repository. CoRR arxiv:1512.03012 (2015)
4. Hua, B.S., et al.: Scenenn: a scene meshes dataset with annotations. In: International Conferene on 3D Vision (3DV'16), pp. 92–101 (2016)
5. Dosovitskiy, A., et al.: CARLA: an open urban driving simulator. In: Annual Conference on Robot Learning, pp. 1–16 (2017)
6. Dai, A., et al.: Scannet: richly-annotated 3d reconstructions of indoor scenes. In: Computer Vision and Pattern Recognition (CVPR'17), pp. 2432–2443 (2017)
7. Hackel, T., et al.: Semantic3d.net: a new large-scale point cloud classification benchmark. In: ISPRS Annals of the Photogrammetry, pp. 91–98 (2017)
8. Graham, B., et al.: 3d semantic segmentation with submanifold sparse convolutional networks. In: CVPR'18, pp. 9224–9232 (2018)
9. Yue, X., et al.: A lidar point cloud generator: from a virtual world to autonomous driving. In: International Conference on Multimedia Retrieval (ICMR'18), pp. 458–464 (2018)
10. Wang, F., et al.: Automatic generation of synthetic lidar point clouds for 3-d data analysis. IEEE Trans. Instrum. Meas. **68**(7), 2671–2673 (2019)
11. Behley, J., et al.: A dataset for semantic segmentation of point cloud sequences. CoRR arxiv:1904.01416 (2019)
12. Mo, K., et al.: PartNet: a large-scale benchmark for fine-grained and hierarchical part-level 3D object understanding. In: Computer Vision and Pattern Recognition (CVPR'19), pp. 909–918 (2019)
13. Liu, Z., et al.: Point-voxel cnn for efficient 3d deep learning. Adv. Neural Inf. Process. Syst. **32** (2019)
14. Uy, M.A., et al.: Revisiting point cloud classification: a new benchmark dataset and classification model on real-world data. In: International Conference on Computer Vision (ICCV'19), pp. 1588–1597 (2019)
15. Manivasagam, S., et al.: Lidarsim: realistic lidar simulation by leveraging the real world (2020)
16. Hu, Q., et al.: Randla-net: efficient semantic segmentation of large-scale point clouds (2020)
17. Xiao, A., et al.: Synlidar: learning from synthetic lidar sequential point cloud for semantic segmentation. CoRR arxiv:2107.05399 (2021)
18. Hu, Q., et al.: Towards semantic segmentation of urban-scale 3d point clouds: a dataset, benchmarks and challenges. In: Computer Vision and Pattern Recognition (CVRP'21), pp. 4977–4987 (2021)
19. Karur, K., et al.: End-to-end synthetic lidar point cloud data generation and deep learning validation. Technical report, SAE Technical Paper (2022)
20. Chen M.. et al., .: Stpls3d: A large-scale synthetic and real aerial photogrammetry 3d point cloud dataset. In: British Mach. Vis. Conf. (BMVC'11). p. 429 (2022)
21. Schult, J., et al.: Controlroom3d: room generation using semantic proxy rooms (2023)
22. Lu, Y., et al.: Machine learning for synthetic data generation: a review. CoRR arxiv:2302.04062 (2023)
23. Lu, G., et al.: A novel method for improving point cloud accuracy in automotive radar object recognition. IEEE Access 78538–78548 (2023)
24. Wu, T., et al.: Omniobject3d: large-vocabulary 3d object dataset for realistic perception, reconstruction and generation. In: Computer Vision and Pattern Recognition (CVPR'23), pp. 803–814 (2023)

25. Vu, T., et al.: Scalable softgroup for 3d instance segmentation on point clouds. IEEE Trans. Pattern Anal. Mach. Intell. **46**(4), 1981–1995 (2023)
26. Zou, L., et al.: Learning geometric consistency and discrepancy for category-level 6d object pose estimation from point clouds. Patt. Recogn. **145**, 109896 (2024)
27. Nassif, J., et al.: Synthetic Data: Revolutionizing the Industrial Metaverse. Springer, Cham (2024). 978-3-031-47560-3
28. Song, Z., et al.: Synthetic datasets for autonomous driving: a survey. IEEE Trans. Intell. Veh. **9**(1), 1847–1864 (2024)
29. NavVis: Navvis vlx 2 (2024). https://www.navvis.com/vlx-2. Accessed 24 Mar 2024
30. Nvidia: Isaac sim (2024). https://developer.nvidia.com/isaac-sim. Accessed 24 Mar 2024
31. Nvidia: Physx sdk (2024). https://developer.nvidia.com/physx-sdk. Accessed 24 Mar 2024
32. Nvidia: Pixar universal scene description (2024). https://developer.nvidia.com/usd. Accessed 24 Mar 2024
33. Yaghi, A., Tekli, J., Kamradt, M., Couturier, R.: 3dgenie: synthetic point clouds for semantic segmentation in realistic virtual environments. Multimedia Tools Appl. 1–33 (2025)

Preserving Intangible Cultural Heritage Through Constructivist Learning in the Metaverse: A Virtual-Reality Experience for Transmitting the Mythological Narratives Around Peirene Fountain

Sajedeh Bijanikia(✉) ⓘ and Makram Mestiri ⓘ

Polytechnic University of Hauts-de-France, 59313 Valenciennes, France
s.bijanikia@gmail.com

Abstract. This study investigates the efficacy of an immersive, constructivist-based virtual reality (VR) intervention for the preservation and transmission of intangible cultural heritage (ICH), focusing on the mythopoetic corpus of the Peirene Fountain in ancient Corinth. The Peirene Fountain embodies a nexus of tangible and intangible heritage, most notably the myth of the nymph Peirene and the taming of Pegasus by Bellerophon. Since the traditional ICH dissemination modalities (e.g., oral narration, static text) are inadequate for engaging contemporary, digitally literate audiences, a VR experience on the Virtual Education Collaborative System (VECOS) platform was designed, leveraging its no-code, 3D objects scan import, AI assisted narrative sequencing, real-time event tracking, and cross device accessibility to create a multi-user, problem-based learning environment. Guided by the Constructivist Theory of Learning, users' prior knowledge is scaffolded and extended through interactive, puzzle-oriented tasks, anchored by 3D reconstructions of key artifacts that facilitate situated, social learning and cognitive apprenticeship. Early validation involved 37 master's students of the "Science and Metaverse Technologies" program, whose unstructured observational data, like scale surveys (mean engagement = 4.2/5; comprehension = 3.8/5), and semi-structured group interviews indicated high levels of immersion, narrative retention, and emergent collaborative behavior. Findings suggest that the constructivist VR framework In VECOS significantly enhanced user engagement, contextualization of mythic narratives, and sustainable ICH transmission. Moreover, the modular, scalable architecture of VECOS suggests broad applicability to diverse heritage contexts, while limitations, such as narrative pacing, multimodal feedback, and hardware accessibility, underscore avenues for iterative refinement and future research.

Keywords: Virtual reality (VR) · Constructivist Theory of Learning (CTL) · Metaverse · Intangible Cultural Heritage (ICH) · Heritage preservation · Peirene Fountain

S. Chen et al. (Eds.): METAVERSE 2025, LNCS 16159, pp. 32–48, 2026.
https://doi.org/10.1007/978-3-032-06323-6_3

1 Introduction

1.1 The Peirene Fountain and Intangible Cultural Heritage

The Peirene Fountain, situated in Corinth and acknowledged by its first excavator Rufus B. Richardson, as "the most important fountain of Greece" [1], has captivated the attention of scholars since its discovery in 1896. With its architectural structure and its long-standing social function as a Corinthian gathering place, this archaeological site serves as a living testament to the tangible and intangible heritage of ancient Corinth. This site is most significantly replete with mythological narratives. According to the Ancient Greek geographer Pausanias in his work "Description of Greece" [2], the legends say that after the Nymph Peirene's son Cenchrias was unintentionally killed by Artemis, she cried in such anguish that she turned into a spring, the one serving as the main water source for the ancient Corinthians. Other stories around the Peirene Fountain include how Bellerophon, the divine Corinthian hero, managed to tame Pegasus, the winged horse, while it was drinking from the fountain [2]. Despite its rich mythical associations, the Peirene Fountain remains relatively unnoted in contemporary public consciousness. At the same time, traditional modes of heritage dissemination, namely, oral storytelling during heritage site visits and written narratives, are insufficient in effectively engaging contemporary audiences with the role and function of mythology in the ancient world.

1.2 Potentials of VR Technology in Preserving ICH

In light of the importance of safeguarding and transmitting intangible cultural heritage "as a mainspring of cultural diversity and a guarantee of sustainable development" [3], transmitting and preserving ICH of ancient cultures and civilizations, such as the Greek Mythology, mainly face certain challenges that are due to their ruptured practice in the contemporary world. Since the most prominent and essential means of cultural transmission is oral storytelling traditions [4], and because the context and objects simultaneously play vital roles in understanding the relevance and socio-cultural functions of ICH, modern technologies such as Virtual Reality (VR) and the metaverse can offer innovative solutions for transmitting intangible heritage, and specifically ancient narratives, in more engaging, accessible, and contextualized environments. In this regard, leveraging the CTL in the process of VR experience design poses a great potential in enhancing the transmission and preservation of ICH, thanks to its user-oriented nature that prioritizes learners' cognitive needs and interests.

1.3 Constructivist Theory of Learning (CTL) for Enhancing Educational Effects of VR Technology

Developed in line with the CTL, and employing the 3D scan of the contemporary Peirene heritage site as well as objects related to the narrative, the designed learning experience aims at immersing the users in the actual setting of the site while exposing them to basic data according to which they can get a sense of the Ancient Greek mythology and construct their knowledge of the myths behind the Peirene Fountain. Being a "purpose-built, multi-user immersive platform offering no-code framework for importing 3D artifacts,

AI-assisted tour creation, real-time event tracking, and cross-device accessibility" [5], VECOS serves as a powerful foreground for realizing the constructivist design objectives of this research. By linking users' prior knowledge to on-site information and extracting the mythical narratives through a scavenger hunt group activity, users engage more deeply with Corinthian intangible heritage. As demonstrated by the early user testing results from evaluations of 4 recruited experts in Cultural Heritage and Human-Metaverse Interaction (HMI), the transmission of intangible cultural heritage to users is realized more sustainably and engagingly by leveraging the VECOS platform to elaborate a constructivist learning experience.

2   Research Objectives and Questions

This study explores how mythological narratives associated with the Peirene Fountain can be preserved and transmitted effectively through immersive virtual environments by leveraging the VECOS platform and implementing the CTL to enhance contextualization and user/learners' engagement. In addressing this goal, the research is guided by specific objectives and questions detailed below:

- Examine how constructivist learning principles can be applied in virtual reality (VR) environments to support heritage transmission.
- Evaluate the effectiveness of VR in preserving and transmitting intangible cultural narratives.
- Investigate user engagement with mythological storytelling within the VECOS platform.

To achieve these objectives, the study addresses the following research questions:

1. How can the constructivist learning framework enhance the transmission of mythological narratives in VR environments?
2. In what ways does the VECOS platform support the preservation of intangible cultural heritage?
3. How do users interact with and interpret mythological stories in immersive virtual settings designed according to the Constructivist Learning principles?

3   Literature Review

By making long-distance and dematerialized communication and information distribution possible, Information and Communication Technologies (ICT) have considerably impacted modes of social interaction and learning. So, the cultural sector, notably the cultural heritage and museums, is one of the major areas affected by the development of these technologies. Due to their responsibility towards society and the public [6], museums and other cultural institutions alike have faced inevitable revisions in their modes of public education, and ICTs played an important role in these revisions due to their novel, engaging, and imaginative nature [7].

3.1 Integration of the Metaverse in the Cultural Sector

Depending on the mode of communication and information transfer embedded in their design, each type of ICT has unique capacities and limitations that determine the context and purpose in which it can be applied. For instance, in the cultural sector, websites and social media tools have the potential to "facilitate communication and marketing … mostly prior to and following a visit" [8], while audio and smart guides as well as touchscreen kiosks are appropriate for improving exhibition or heritage site design [8]. Despite the significant improvements these types of ICTs have brought to the quality of the public's interaction with cultural and heritage institutions, the mentioned examples mainly rely on passive, rather than active, participation in which curators and heritage professionals define what information the public learn through ICTs [9]. In contrast, more recent technologies such as Augmented and Virtual Reality offer users' greater freedom and interaction in their experience and learning process. By facilitating contextualization [10–12], freedom of movement [13], and creative interactions [14, 15], these technologies present extended potential for employing more user/audience-oriented learning theories in cultural experiences.

In current studies on AR and VR integration in the cultural sector, two of the most prominent areas of concentration emerged: gamification [16–19] and edutainment [20–23]. While such studies have successfully kept the momentum of integrating emerging technologies in the cultural sector, they have approached the aim of enhancing the public's access, interaction, and engagement with cultural institutions in somewhat curator/educator-oriented tendencies. In other words, although it cannot be argued that these designs are completely under the influence of what Recupero [24] calls a "positivism-behaviorist approach", their educational inclinations, are at very best, still hierarchical; putting the educator- in this case, designers- on top of the pedagogical pyramid, and with the mission of "transmitting" predetermined knowledge to the learners to "absorb" [25]. In several cases of these studies, one can even contend that a clear theoretical framework or learning theory is missing in their process of VR experience design, which, consequently, affects the depth of learners' engagement and knowledge acquisition [16, 17, 22].

3.2 Toward a Constructivist Framework for ICH Transmission in the Metaverse

Through the analysis of scholarly works on cultural heritage VR experiences that leverage gamification and edutainment, it is demonstrated that they have mainly overlooked how traditional modes of ICH transmission can be integrated into the metaverse to open innovative pathways for enhancing heritage preservation [26]. This is while, according to anthropological and cultural heritage studies, the traditional methods of transmitting ICH in societies are deeply embedded in daily life and social structures [3]. As Hou et al. [27] have discussed, "Intangible heritage is inherently a living entity, a cultural space that incorporates a know-how process that is anecdotal, oral, embodied, shared, and in evolutionary adaptation to its various audiences". In this regard, it can be argued that the development of new technologies enables ICH, as a living entity, to evolve by extending its long-standing practices into the metaverse through the participation of users- humans who have traditionally been the carriers and transmitters of ICH in real life. These individuals have engaged with heritage through anecdotal narratives, oral storytelling, embodied practices, and the communal sharing of knowledge [28]. As such, humankind brings into the metaverse a reservoir of prior knowledge and experience rooted in traditional modes of ICH transmission, which have historically been embedded in daily life and social structures.

This embodied understanding constitutes a vital asset for extending ICH transmission within virtual environments, particularly when designers consciously integrate it into their frameworks. This integration is crucial for forms of ICH, like ancient mythological traditions, that have lost their original contexts and means of generational transmission due to socio-historical ruptures [29]. These traditions, once passed down through elders and reinforced by material contexts that conveyed their cultural and social significance, now face challenges due to historical interruptions. The metaverse offers a unique potential to re-create these lost contexts and reimagine intergenerational transmission in novel ways. By designing immersive and meaningful virtual experiences, it is possible to preserve and transmit such intangible wisdom to younger generations in a more accessible, engaging, and culturally resonant manner. Due to the intricate and intertwined nature of intangible cultural heritage components, the proposition of integrating their traditional modes of transmission in the metaverse could be convenient in terms of connecting this experience to what the users had previously known about these ICH.

As previously discussed, while other theories, such as behaviorism, cognitivism, experiential learning, or connectivism, offer valuable approaches to instruction, they present limitations in addressing the socially situated, interpretive, and narrative-rich nature of ICH. Behaviorist and cognitivist models emphasize linear, instructor-driven content delivery and knowledge acquisition, which misalign with the oral, dialogic, and symbolic dynamics through which ICH is traditionally transmitted. In contrast, CTL foregrounds learner agency, prior knowledge activation, and situated learning within meaningful contexts- principles that resonate with how ICH was passed intergenerationally. Furthermore, the immersive, multi-user affordances of platforms like VECOS lend themselves naturally to CTL's core principles, such as cognitive apprenticeship, problem-based learning, and legitimate peripheral participation. This alignment ensures that the design of VR heritage experiences is not merely engaging but pedagogically grounded in a theory of learning that honors both the medium and the message.

4   Methodology and Implementation

4.1   Case Study Site: The Peirene Fountain

Myths, gods, and mythical creatures were not just elements of storytelling in the ancient era. Instead, they were foundational to understanding the world, guiding moral conduct, legitimizing political power, and uniting communities through shared beliefs and practices. In this regard, the Peirene Fountain in ancient Corinth exemplifies how mythology is intertwined with various aspects of social life, namely religion, moral frameworks, politics, education, identity, art, and traditions. For instance, the myth of Peirine, who transformed into a fountain due to profound grief over her son's accidental death by Artemis, conveys a powerful narrative of mourning, maternal love, and transformation. On the other hand, it not only provided moral lessons for the ancient Corinthians, but also offers us an understanding of the importance of water resources for the ancient Greek settlements, to such an extent that they were mythicized to enhance their appreciation.

4.2 The VECOS Platform

According to the previous study on the capabilities of the VECOS platform in fostering social interaction [5], and based on the objectives of the present research, the following list demonstrates how VECOS features are relevant to preserving intangible cultural heritage through a constructivist VR experience around the Peirene Fountain:

Fig. 1. The school room: first step to explore the fountain of Peirene in VECOS

1. *Multi-user Immersive Environment:* Enables multiple users to participate simultaneously in the VR experience, fostering social learning and interaction, which aligns well with the social nature of ICH transmission (see Fig. 1.).
2. *No-code Framework for Importing and programming interaction of 3D Artifacts:* Allows easy integration of 3D scans of the Peirene Fountain site and related heritage objects without requiring extensive programming skills, hence, facilitating contextualization.
3. *AI-assisted Tour Creation:* Although the present VR experience is not designed in a tour format, this feature supports the development of narrative sequences that highlight the intertwined mythological stories and heritage information in an engaging and structured manner.
4. *Real-time Event Tracking:* Provides data on user interactions and movements within the VR space, useful for analyzing engagement, learning behaviors, and the effectiveness of the CTL-based design.
5. *Cross-device Accessibility:* Ensures the VR experience can be accessed on various devices, making it more accessible and inclusive to diverse user groups and promoting wider dissemination of the intangible cultural heritage content.
6. *Support for User-driven Learning Activities:* Facilitates active participation through interactive group activities that encourage users to explore and construct knowledge collaboratively, directly applying constructivist learning principles.
7. *Immersive 3D Environment Rendering:* Delivers a highly realistic reconstruction of the Peirene Fountain environment, enabling users to experience the spatial and material context crucial for understanding and appreciating the intangible heritage.
8. *Integration of Multimedia Content:* Supports embedding audios, videos, visual, and textual information, which can be used to enrich the mythological narratives and provide layered learning experiences.

4.3 Constructivist Learning Principles

The CTL relies on the core belief that knowledge resides in the mind and is constructed by the learner. It denies the absolute, independent knowledge that exists outside of the subject/learner, and emphasizes how every individual's reservoir of prior knowledge affects their understanding of the subject at hand. In Hein's words [25], it allows individuals to "make connections between the known and the new". Through this description, the relevance of such an understanding of knowledge and theory of education to cultural entities such as the ICH is apparent. Within the social framework of every region, individuals and communities practice and pass on the elements of ICH, which have initially been developed according to humankind's understanding of the world. In this theory, the process of designing a learning experience consists of the following components:

- Situated learning
- Problem-based learning
- Self-orientation
- Cognitive apprenticeship
- Legitimate peripheral participation
- Top-down instruction
- Formative assessment

4.4 Object Selection and Narrative Design

Based on the CTL principles, the design of the VR experience required careful identification of both tangible heritage objects and their associated mythological narratives. This section details the process by which key physical elements of the Peirene Fountain and its environs were selected for inclusion, and how the sequence and framing of mythic content were structured to support active, learner-driven knowledge construction.

Criteria for Object Selection. *Authenticity and Contextual Relevance.* Following CTL's situated learning tenet, objects were chosen for their direct ties to the fountain's function and mythic symbolism. Primary among these is the fountain structure itself, its stone basin, piped water channel, and frescoed springhouse walls, all embodying both the material and social dimensions of Peirene's myths.

Narrative Anchors. Secondary artifacts, including the sculptural representation of Pegasus and the painting on Cenchrias's story, were incorporated as "narrative anchors" to serve dual purposes: (a) as visual cues prompting learners to recall or discover specific mythic episodes, and (b) as focal points around which interactive tasks (puzzles, clue gathering, or waypoint-based dialogues) are built. Aligned with CTL's emphasis on problem-based learning, these objects prompt learners to explore the cause-and-effect relationships underlying each myth (e.g., why Bellerophon sought Pegasus at Peirene) and to construct their own interpretations of symbolic meaning.

Facilitation of Social Interaction. Recognizing CTL's legitimate peripheral participation tenet, objects encouraging collaborative discovery were prioritized. For example, a holistically-scanned shard of a plaque conveys offerings made by ancient Corinthians; multiple users must work together to reassemble the fractured inscriptions, thereby coaxing small- group discussion about the fountain's societal role. By selecting such objects, designers create nodes of social engagement that mirror traditional, communal, oral storytelling practices.

Mapping Mythological Narratives. *Sequence Alignment with Constructivist Principles.* The authors first compiled a corpus of documented mythic episodes linked to Peirene. Each narrative fragment was then situated in a mapped network of myths, ensuring that foundational motifs (e.g., grief and transformation) scaffolded subsequent, more complex themes (e.g., heroism and flight). This ordering adheres to CTL's tenet of connecting new information to learners' prior knowledge: users encounter simpler narrative threads first (e.g., identifying the spring's origin), which primes them to tackle richer, multilayered stories later (e.g., Pegasus's divine symbolism).

Branching Narrative Paths. To promote self-orientation, a branching path design was implemented. At each major object node (e.g., the fountain's spout, the Pegasus sculpture, the votive plaque), users choose among multiple "clue trails." For instance, upon reaching the sculpted Pegasus hoof, participants might elect to (a) solve a riddle revealing Pegasus's birth, or (b) engage in a collaborative memory activity about its lineage. Each choice leads to a different mini-narrative, yet all paths reconverge at nexus points where overarching lessons about mortal-divine interaction or the symbolic value of water are underscored. This aligns with CTL's advocacy for offering learners control over their inquiry and encouraging knowledge construction through choice.

Integration of Multimedia Layers. Each object's narrative node is enhanced with multimedia annotations: short audio and video recitations of Pausanias's text (translated), animated overlays depicting mythic events, and interactive text prompts asking users to hypothesize why ancient Corinthians honored Peirene in specific rituals. Embedding these layers onto tangible 3D models through VECOS's support for multimedia integration ensures that learners can engage multiple senses when constructing meaning- an approach in line with CTL's cognitive apprenticeship and multimodal sense-making.

Designing Interactive Tasks Around Objects. *Scavenger Hunt Structure.* Central to the narrative design is a problem-based scavenger hunt that unfolds spatially: learners must locate designated "Clue Crystals" (small, glowing markers) placed at selected object sites (e.g., beside the fountain spout, atop a carved relief). Each Clue Crystal houses a narrative prompt, such as "Why did Artemis's arrow stray?" or "What does Pegasus's first appearance signify?", that can only be unlocked by solving a short puzzle (matching symbolic icons or assembling shattered pottery pieces). This aligns with CTL's problem-based learning tenet, positioning users as active investigators seeking contextualized knowledge rather than passive recipients of prepackaged facts (see Fig. 2.).

Cognitive Apprenticeship and Scaffolding. Early in the experience, tasks are scaffolded closely: a virtual guide avatar provides breadcrumbs (e.g., highlighting a relevant fresco panel) (See Fig. 3.). As users progress, prompts become less directive, requiring learners to draw on accumulated insights. For example, after identifying the cause of Peirene's metamorphosis, the next stage prompts: "Consider why water, rather than stone, became Peirene's enduring form. How might this transformation reflect Corinthian values?" By gradually shifting responsibility from system guidance to self-driven conjecture,

Fig. 2. Teleportation from the school room to 3D scanned architecture in VECOS.

the design mirrors CTL's cognitive apprenticeship model; apprentices observe and imitate at first, then progressively take charge of problem-solving. Embedding Formative Assessment. At each narrative node, user inputs (answers, puzzle solutions, or hypothesis submissions) are logged in real time. When incorrect or incomplete, contextual hints appear, prompting reflection rather than simply revealing the answer. This formative feedback loop encourages metacognition: learners assess their understanding of mythic causality (e.g., linking grief with metamorphosis) before moving on. The system's real-time event tracking supports such assessments by capturing interaction data that can later inform iterative refinement of tasks and narrative pacing.

Fig. 3. Guided tour with the AI-powered Avatar "Baya" in VECOS

Ensuring Cultural and Pedagogical Coherence. *Preserving Oral Tradition Dynamics.* Although the VR environment is digital, narrative delivery imitates the communal feel of traditional oral storytelling. Key objects are "staging areas" where virtual avatars recount brief episodes in first-person voice (e.g., "I am Peirene; hear my sorrow…"). These moments are interspersed with user prompts, stimulating dialogue among participants. By recreating the give-and-take of oral discourse, the design honors intangible heritage practices while embedding them in a constructivist framework that foregrounds learner agency.

Balancing Depth and Accessibility. Recognizing that some users may be unfamiliar with Greek myths, narrative content is layered by complexity. Basic facts are introduced early via labeled diagrams or glossary pop-ups. More advanced themes (e.g., the moral implications of divine intervention) require users to engage in higher-order tasks, such as comparing the Peirene narrative with other Greek metamorphosis myths. This layered approach preserves CTL's commitment to meeting learners at their starting points:

novices gain confidence through simpler engagements, while advanced learners pursue deeper thematic connections.

Cultural Sensitivity and Accuracy. All object labels, mythic reconstructions, and audio scripts were vetted by two independent experts in Greek mythology and heritage ethics to ensure fidelity to both archaeological evidence and oral tradition scholarship. The narrative design explicitly acknowledges areas of scholarly debate (e.g., multiple versions of Peirene's story) by surfacing alternate "what-if" branches, thereby modeling how interpretive variation is a natural part of heritage knowledge construction.

5   Early Testing Results

5.1   Participant Selection and Context

To examine the effectiveness of our Constructivist approach in transmitting the Peirene Fountain's mythical narratives, we conducted an early user test with a cohort of 37 master's students enrolled in the "Science and Metaverse Technologies" program, none of whom had prior familiarity with the Peirene Fountain or its associated myths. All participants were in their second semester of the curriculum, so they possessed a foundational understanding of digital-heritage concepts and basic VR interaction skills. These characteristics made them suitable for testing the digital interaction and usability of the prototype. However, as all participants were digital technology students with prior VR exposure, this sample may introduce a bias toward more favorable perceptions of immersive environments. Future evaluations will expand to include more demographically diverse groups such as tourists, heritage site visitors, older adults, and secondary-school students to increase generalizability and cultural representativeness. After giving them an overview of the objectives behind this VR experience, they engaged with the VR space without specific prompts. This enabled the observation of participants' interactions without the need for intervention.

5.2   Data Collection Methodology

To capture nuanced feedback on user engagement and narrative comprehension, we employed a mixed-methods approach tailored to exploratory studies:

Unstructured Observation. During a 20-min session in a dedicated VR lab, participants navigated the Peirene Fountain environment wearing standard VR headsets. Two facilitators silently observed each student's interactions, tracking how they discovered "Clue Crystals", manipulated artifacts (e.g., attempting to reassemble the votive plaque), and consulted multimedia annotations. Observers took field notes on patterns of behavior (e.g., hesitation at decision nodes, collaborative gestures when multiple users joined the same space), without guiding once the session began.

Structured Survey Instruments. Immediately after the VR session, all 37 students completed a 12-item Likert-scale questionnaire (with answers rated $1 =$ Strongly Disagree to $5 =$ Strongly Agree) assessing:

- Engagement (e.g., "I felt motivated to explore each object because it encouraged me to solve puzzles")
- Comprehension (e.g., "I can accurately recount the myth of Peirene's transformation after completing the tasks")
- Usability (e.g., "Navigating the 3D environment felt intuitive")
- Perceived Authenticity (e.g., "The 3D artifacts and audio narration felt faithful to what I imagine the real Peirene Fountain might be")

Semi-structured Group Interviews. Participants were then divided into four groups (8–10 students each) for 15-min, semi-structured group interviews discussing:

- Which interactive tasks best helped them understand the mythical narratives
- Points of confusion or narrative gaps
- How the social/collaborative aspects (e.g., multiplayer presence, shared puzzle solving) influenced their learning
- Suggestions for improving object selection or narrative clarity.

Quantitative Results

- Engagement: Mean score = 4.2 (SD = 0.6). Over 80% of students agreed or strongly agreed that the problem-based tasks (scavenger hunt, puzzle assembly) motivated them to seek narrative details actively.
- Comprehension: Mean score = 3.8 (SD = 0.7). Approximately 75% reported being able to accurately recount at least two core mythic episodes (Peirene's metamorphosis and Pegasus's origin) after the session; 60% felt they could explain the symbolic significance of water in the myth.
- Usability: Mean score = 4.0 (SD = 0.5). Most students found navigation straight-forward, though 20% noted occasional uncertainty when multiple decision nodes appeared in quick succession.
- Perceived Authenticity: Mean score = 3.9 (SD = 0.8). While many praised the fidelity of the 3D-scanned fountain and sculptural details, around 25% suggested that higher-resolution textures or additional environmental cues (e.g., ambient sound of flowing water) would enhance authenticity (see Fig. 4.).

5.3 Qualitative Insights

Positive Observations

- Active Meaning-Making: Students frequently paused at narrative anchors (e.g., Pegasus sculpture) to hypothesize mythological context aloud before unlocking the next clue. Thus, learners used prior understanding of Greek myths to fill narrative gaps.
- Collaborative Discovery: Even though the test was not explicitly structured for teamwork, the presence of multiple avatars in the same virtual space led students to form

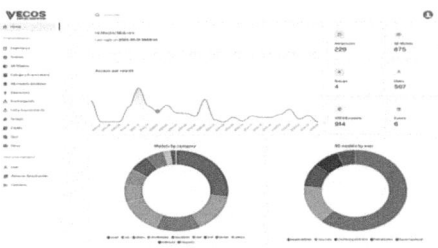

Fig. 4. Real-time quantitative statistics from VECOS immersions metaverse experiences

partnerships in solving puzzles, comparing annotations, and debating interpretation of symbols. This mirrored traditional communal storytelling, reinforcing the CTL goal of situated, social learning.

- Ease of Task Progression: The scaffolding in early tasks (e.g., guided highlighting of objects) enabled participants with limited prior mythological knowledge to grasp foundational narrative elements quickly, building confidence for more complex challenges later in the experience.

Areas for Improvement. Based on participant feedback and observed engagement, several enhancements are proposed for future iterations. First, user navigation through branching narrative paths revealed occasional confusion at nexus points, suggesting the need for subtle visual cues (e.g., directional markers or glowing indicators) to guide progression while preserving user autonomy. Second, multiple students expressed interest in deeper contextual background on Corinthian cultural practices and myth variants. To address this, optional "context capsules" will be introduced- short, unlockable multimedia layers providing additional cultural, ritual, or historical depth.

Third, the current reliance on visual and textual cues occasionally slowed comprehension, particularly for complex puzzles. As such, we propose integrating subtle auditory cues (e.g., a soft chime upon puzzle resolution) and haptic feedback (e.g., controller vibration for successful interactions) to enhance multimodal learning. Finally, user reports of mild disorientation suggest incorporating "rest zones" or short reflection pauses between major narrative branches to reduce cognitive load and VR fatigue.

Other propositions are:

- Narrative Pacing: Several participants reported that certain decision nodes, especially nexus points, appeared in rapid succession, leading to confusion about choosing next clues. They recommended clearer signposting (e.g., subtle visual arrows or breadcrumb indicators) to guide progression without diluting autonomy.
- Depth of Context: While students could identify the core mythic episodes, some expressed a desire for additional background on Corinthian cultural practices (e.g., why local worship of Peirene persisted after classical antiquity). Incorporating optional "context capsules" (short, unlockable video clips or 360° panoramas) was suggested to deepen understanding for those seeking richer context.
- Multimodal Feedback: Some participants noted that relying on visual and textual cues sometimes slowed their comprehension, particularly when deciphering riddles.

They proposed integrating subtle auditory cues (e.g., a soft gong when a puzzle is solved) or haptic feedback (controller vibration) to reinforce task completion.

• Accessibility Considerations: Although all students had prior VR exposure, 15% felt mildly disoriented during prolonged immersion, suggesting that optional "rest points" (breaks or a neutral landing platform) could reduce VR fatigue.

6 Dicussion

6.1 Effectiveness of the VR Constructivist Approach in ICH Preservation

The constructivist VR experience of Peirene Fountain demonstrates clear advantages over traditional methods of transmitting intangible cultural heritage. The VR constructivist design compels users to engage directly with the spatial and material context of the fountain, linking mythical narratives to tangible 3D artifacts and environmental cues. Participants reported that navigating the reconstructed fountain, locating narrative clues during the scavenger hunt, and interacting with multimedia prompts fostered a higher level of personal engagement with the myths. However, the overall compre-hension score (mean = 3.8/5) suggests that while learners retained core narrative ele-ments, more nuanced or symbolic dimensions- such as moral themes or mythic archeypes-may require additional scaffolding or extended exposure time. This high-lights the value of refining narrative pacing and layering content for varying levels of familiarity with Greek mythology. By situating learning tasks within a realistic, multi-user environment, the VR model enacts several core constructivist principles, situated learning, problem-based exploration, and legitimate peripheral participation, thereby enabling learners to construct meaning actively. Moreover, the social dimension of the experience (multiple users' collaboration) reintroduces the communal, oral-transmission aspects of ICH. As a result, the VR experience not only preserves the content of Peirene's myths but also reactivates the social processes through which those myths were traditionally transmitted. It is also important to note that this study lacked a control group using traditional interpretive formats, such as guided tours or printed narratives. While participants reported increased engagement and retention within the immersive setting, the absence of a comparative condition limits claims about the specific pedagogical advantage of the VR experience. Future research will adopt a mixed method comparative design to more precisely assess the differential impact of constructivist VR environments versus conventional heritage learning modalities.

6.2 Potential for Scalability

The modular, no-code architecture of the VECOS platform and its support for importing photogrammetric 3D scans and layered multimedia content creates a scalable framework for applying this constructivist approach to other cultural heritage sites. Any heritage location that can be 3D scanned can be embedded within VECOS and enriched with narrative nodes, interactive tasks, and collaborative learning activities. For instance, Greek sites such as the Sanctuary of Apollo at Delphi or the site of Eleusis could adopt a similar workflow: (1) capture high-resolution scans of architectural remains, (2) map out mythological or folk narratives tied to those remains, and (3) create scavenger-hunt tasks or problem-based modules that guide users through contextually relevant knowledge construction.Beyond Greece, intangible practices, such as traditional dances in Bali or oral epics in West Africa, could be represented by combining 360° video, avatar-mediated interactions, and annotation hotspots within VR, all governed by constructivist design. Importantly, VECOS's cross-device accessibility ensures that participants need not possess top-tier VR headsets; Desktop viewers and mobile-VR options can broaden reach. In terms of resource efficiency, once a template for narrative integration and user-driven activities is established, content creators can replicate it with minimal additional programming, thus reducing development costs. The outcome is a replicable, sustainable blueprint for digital-heritage preservation that can be tailored to diverse geographic, cultural, and narrative contexts.

6.3 Limitations Encountered

Despite promising early findings, the following limitations emerged: First, although participants' feedback was uniformly positive, their insights may not reflect the responses of general audiences. Broadening testing to include tourists and local community members will be essential to validate generalizability. Technical constraints-such as occasional frame-rate drops in high-polygon scenes, inconsistent avatar locomotion, and limited haptic feedback-were noted to detract from immersive flow. These disruptions likely imposed additional cognitive load, particularly during more complex narrative puzzles or spatial exploration tasks. In turn, they may have impacted narrative continuity and learning efficacy. As such, future refinement of system performance and real-time responsiveness will be essential to fully realize the cognitive potential of constructivist VR environments. Some participants noted that if graphical fidelity does not match the user's expectations (e.g., highly detailed frescoes versus simplified textures), it may undermine the perceived authenticity of the heritage site. Third, the current narrative scope is confined to a subset of Peirene's myths; other aspects, such as regional variations of the story or adjacent archaeological elements like the underground tunnels are not yet integrated. This limits the comprehensiveness of ICH transmission. Finally, although the constructivist framework encourages user autonomy, it may prove challenging for participants with no prior knowledge of Greek mythology; scaffolding more introductory content or guided tutorials might be necessary. Given the 20-min duration of the VR session, it is likely that only surface-level retention was achieved for certain participants. While early comprehension scores indicate moderate narrative uptake, a longitudinal follow-up-administered several days or weeks post-experience-could provide deeper insight into the sustainability of engagement and learning. Such delayed assessments would also help evaluate the resonance of mythic symbolism beyond initial exposure.

7 Conclusion

This study has demonstrated that an immersive, constructivist driven VR intervention can substantially enhance the preservation and transmission of intangible cultural heritage (ICH) by recontextualizing ancient mythopoetic narratives within a user-centered, problem-based learning environment. By leveraging the VECOS platform, we created a multi-user VR experience anchored around the mythological corpus of the Peirene Fountain, one of ancient Corinth's most significant ICH. Guided by CTL, the experience situated learners in an authentic reconstruction of the fountain's material environment, where interactive, puzzle-oriented tasks scaffolded users' prior knowledge and catalyzed collaborative inquiry.

Early empirical validation with 37 master's level participants in "Science and Metaverse Technologies" revealed robust levels of engagement (mean = 4.2/5) and narrative comprehension (mean = 3.8/5), as well as emergent social dynamics that mirror traditional oral transmission processes. Qualitative feedback underscored how the problem-based "scavenger hunt" structure and multimedia annotations facilitated situated social learning and cognitive apprenticeship tenets of constructivist pedagogy. Furthermore, the modular architecture of VECOS proved highly scalable: the workflow of 3D scanning, narrative mapping, and interactive task design could be replicated for other heritage sites, enabling a vessel for ICH transmission across diverse cultural contexts.

Nonetheless, several limitations must be acknowledged. Narrative pacing suffered when branching paths reconverged, suggesting a need for enhanced signposting and progressive scaffolding. Multimodal feedback (e.g., haptic cues, ambient sound) was required for reinforcing learning and mitigating VR fatigue. Hardware accessibility remains a barrier for users lacking high-end headsets, indicating that continued cross-device optimization is essential for equitable dissemination. Finally, the present narrative scope is confined to a subset of Peirene's myths; a more exhaustive inclusion of regional variants and adjacent archaeological (e.g., underground tunnels) would further enrich ICH transmission.

Future work will therefore focus on iterative refinements along four fronts: (1) Narrative Expansion, integrating additional mythic threads and optional "context capsules" to deepen cultural contextualization; (2) Multimodal Enhancement, embedding auditory and haptic feedback to reinforce formative assessment and minimize disorientation; (3) Accessibility & Inclusivity, developing "rest points" and mobile VR adaptations to broaden participation among non-expert audiences; and (4) Evaluation conducting large scale, longitudinal studies with diverse user cohorts (e.g., local communities, tourists, secondary education students) to assess knowledge retention and attitudinal shifts over time.

References

1. Robinson, B.A.: Histories of Peirene: A Corinthian fountain in three Millennia. American School of Classical Studies at Athens, Princeton (2011)
2. Pausanias: Description of Greece. Harvard University Press (1964)
3. Text of the Convention for the Safeguarding of the Intangible Cultural Heritage - UNESCO Intangible Cultural Heritage. https://ich.unesco.org/en/convention. Accessed 08 June 2025
4. Oral traditions and expressions including language as a vehicle of the intangible cultural heritage - UNESCO Intangible Cultural Heritage. https://ich.unesco.org/en/oral-traditions-and-expressions-00053. Accessed 08 June 2025
5. Mestiri, M., Khadhar, M., Huftier, A., Fergombe, A.: Fostering social interaction variability in the metaverse: a case study of the museum of L'Avesnois in fourmies. Heritage **8**, 171 (2025). https://doi.org/10.3390/heritage8050171

6. Museum Definition. https://icom.museum/en/resources/standards-guidelines/museum-defini tion/. Accessed 08 June 2025

7. Barbosa, C.C.: Innovation in museums through the use of ICTs (2013). https://www.duo.uio.no/handle/10852/35928

8. Mohammed, S.N., Jamhawi, M., Rashid, M.: Effectiveness of using information and communication technology in developing museum exhibitions: the case of the Sharjah museums. ISTRAŽIVANJA J. Hist. Res. 191–212 (2022). https://doi.org/10.19090/i.2022.33.191-212

9. Karakuş Yılmaz, T., Meral, E., Başcı Namlı, Z.: A systematic review of the pedagogical roles of technology in ICT-assisted museum learning studies. Educ. Inf. Technol. **29**, 10069–10103 (2024). https://doi.org/10.1007/s10639-023-12208-3

10. Lacko, J.: Cultural heritage objects in education by virtual and augmented reality. In: tom Dieck, M.C. and Jung, T. (eds.) Augmented Reality and Virtual Reality: The Power of AR and VR for Business, pp. 175–187. Springer, Cham (2019). https://doi.org/10.1007/978-3-030-06246-0_13

11. Ahdhianto, E., Barus, Y.K., Thohir, M.A.: Augmented reality as a game changer in experiential learning: exploring its role cultural education for elementary schools. J. Pedagog. Res. **9**, 296–313 (2025). https://doi.org/10.33902/JPR.202533573

12. Cunha, C.R., Mendonça, V., Moreira, A., Gomes, J.P., Carvalho, A.: Using virtual reality in museums to bridge the gap between material heritage and the interpretation of its immaterial context. In: Abreu, A., Liberato, D., and Garcia Ojeda, J.C. (eds.) Advances in Tourism, Technology and Systems, pp. 397–408. Springer, Singapore (2022). https://doi.org/10.1007/978-981-19-1040-1_34

13. Nofal, E., Elhanafi, A.M., Hameeuw, H., Moere, A.V.: Architectural contextualization of heritage museum artifacts using augmented reality. Stud. Digit. Herit. **2**, 42–67 (2018). https://doi.org/10.14434/sdh.v2i1.24500

14. Wang, A., Thompson, M., Uz-Bilgin, C., Klopfer, E.: Authenticity, interactivity, and collaboration in virtual reality games: best practices and lessons learned. Front. Virtual Real. **2** (2021). https://doi.org/10.3389/frvir.2021.734083

15. Yang, S., Gao, Z., Mogavi, R.H., Hui, P., Braud, T.: Tangible web: an interactive immersion virtual RealityCreativity system that travels across reality. In: Proceedings of the ACM Web Conference 2023, pp. 3915–3922 (2023). https://doi.org/10.1145/3543507.3587432

16. Li, Z., Zhang, Q., Xu, J., Li, C., Yang, X.: Gamification of virtual museum curation: a case study of Chinese bronze wares. Herit. Sci. **12**, 1–18 (2024). https://doi.org/10.1186/s40494-024-01464-2

17. Liu, Y., Lin, Y., Shi, R., Luo, Y., Liang, H.-N.: RelicVR: a virtual reality game for active exploration of archaeological relics. In: Extended Abstracts of the 2021 Annual Symposium on Computer-Human Interaction in Play. pp. 326–332. Association for Computing Machinery, New York (2021). https://doi.org/10.1145/3450337.3483507

18. Hammady, R., Ma, M., Temple, N.: Augmented reality and gamification in heritage museums. In: Marsh, T., Ma, M., Oliveira, M.F., Baalsrud Hauge, J., and Göbel, S. (eds.) Serious Games, pp. 181–187. Springer, Cham (2016). https://doi.org/10.1007/978-3-319-45841-0_17

19. Bujari, A., Ciman, M., Gaggi, O., Palazzi, C.E.: Using gamification to discover cultural heritage locations from geo-tagged photos. Pers. Ubiquitous Comput. **21**, 235–252 (2017). https://doi.org/10.1007/s00779-016-0989-6

20. Dima, M., Daylamani-Zad, D., Lympouridis, V.: Mixed reality heritage performance as a decolonising tool for heritage sites (2024). http://arxiv.org/abs/2404.07348, https://doi.org/10.48550/arXiv.2404.07348

21. Zhang, J., Wan Yahaya, W.A.J., Sanmugam, M.: The impact of immersive technologies on cultural heritage: a bibliometric study of VR, AR, and MR applications. Sustainability. **16**, 6446 (2024). https://doi.org/10.3390/su16156446

22. Yuen, S., Yaoyuneyong, G., Johnson, E.: Augmented reality: an overview and five directions for AR in education. J. Educ. Technol. Dev. Exch. JETDE. **4** (2011). https://doi.org/10.18785/jetde.0401.10
23. Vert, S., et al.: User evaluation of a multi-platform digital storytelling concept for cultural heritage. Mathematics. **9**, 2678 (2021). https://doi.org/10.3390/math9212678
24. Recupero, A., Talamo, A., Triberti, S., Modesti, C.: Bridging museum mission to visitors' experience: activity, meanings, interactions, technology. Front. Psychol. **10** (2019). https://doi.org/10.3389/fpsyg.2019.02092
25. Hein, G.E.: Learning in the Museum. Routledge, London (2002). https://doi.org/10.4324/9780203028322
26. Gaitatzes, A., Christopoulos, D., Roussou, M.: Reviving the past: cultural heritage meets virtual reality. In: Proceedings of the 2001 Conference on Virtual Reality, Archeology, and Cultural Heritage. pp. 103–110. Association for Computing Machinery, New York (2001). https://doi.org/10.1145/584993.585011
27. Hou, Y., Kenderdine, S., Picca, D., Egloff, M., Adamou, A.: Digitizing intangible cultural heritage embodied: state of the art. J. Comput. Cult. Herit. **15**, 55:1–55:20 (2022). https://doi.org/10.1145/3494837
28. Transmission - UNESCO Intangible Cultural Heritage. https://ich.unesco.org/en/transmission-00078. Accessed 08 June 2025
29. Dundes, A.: Sacred Narrative: Readings in the Theory of Myth. University of California Press (1984)

Application of Artificial Intelligence and Metaverse Technologies in Biopharmaceutical Vocational Education: Trends and Practical Pathways

Fan Zhang[1], Jian Lyu[2(✉)], and Yanli Ge[3]

[1] Hubei Vocational College of Bio-Technology, Wuhan 430070, Hubei, China
[2] Shenzhen Urban Transport Planning Center Co., Ltd., Shenzhen 518052, Guangdong, China
`jian.lv@hotmail.com`
[3] Jiangxi Biotech Vocational College, Nanchang 330200, Jiangxi, China

Abstract. As the biopharmaceutical industry rapidly develops, the demand for highly skilled interdisciplinary professionals is becoming increasingly urgent. This paper explores the deep integration of Artificial Intelligence (AI) and Metaverse technologies in the field of biopharmaceutical vocational education, analyzing the key pathways through which they drive transformation of teaching models, including innovative practices such as immersive virtual laboratories, Bioprocess Digital Twin (BPDT) technology, and virtual GMP compliance training. The study indicates that these technological approaches not only resolve issues of limited resources, delayed feedback, and insufficient practice in traditional teaching models, but also achieve a close integration of theoretical knowledge and practical operation, significantly enhancing students' systems thinking, hands-on skills, and compliance awareness. The findings emphasize that advancing the dual driving forces of technological empowerment and industry-education integration will be the key pathway for China's vocational education to achieve high-quality development. Future research should also pay attention to data security and AI ethics in digital transformation, and conduct empirical studies to verify the actual effectiveness of different approaches.

Keywords: Biopharmaceutical Vocational Education · Artificial Intelligence · Metaverse · Digital Twin · Industry-Education Integration · Digital Transformation

1 Introduction

As a core pillar of the nation's strategic emerging industries, the biopharmaceutical industry is experiencing unprecedented changes in its talent development needs. According to the China Biopharmaceutical Industry Development Report (2023), by 2030 the talent gap in high-skill positions in the biopharmaceutical field will exceed one million, spanning areas such as vaccines, plasma products, antibody drugs, and cell therapy [1]. The

S. Chen et al. (Eds.): METAVERSE 2025, LNCS 16159, pp. 49–62, 2026.
https://doi.org/10.1007/978-3-032-06323-6_4

competencies required for biopharmaceutical positions exhibit highly interdisciplinary characteristics: they include core practical skills like aseptic operations and bioprocess control; digital analytical skills such as bioinformatics and automation control; and compliance awareness of Good Manufacturing Practice (GMP) quality standards and Food and Drug Administration (FDA)/European Medicines Agency (EMA) regulations, supplemented by soft skills like communication, teamwork, and innovative thinking. Together, these multi-faceted abilities form a competency framework for the workforce [2].

However, the current vocational education system mainly centers on static lab teaching and single-skill training, which cannot meet the aforementioned requirements for flexible, systematic, and interdisciplinary abilities. In particular, in training for high biosafety level and extremely costly processes (such as fermentation, chromatography, lyophilization) and rigorous GMP compliance, traditional teaching models – due to low accessibility of training resources and insufficient hands-on practice – are facing severe challenges [3]. Therefore, exploring new educational models that are digitalized, modular, and integrate industry–academia–research has become a critical initiative for promoting the sustainable development of the bioeconomy.

The rapid development of Artificial Intelligence (AI) and Metaverse technologies is providing new technical breakthroughs for the digital transformation of vocational education. The Metaverse uses immersive technologies such as Virtual Reality (VR)/Augmented Reality (AR) to construct virtual environments that can simulate high-risk, complex processes, while AI endows these virtual environments with intelligent feedback, real-time assessment, and personalized guidance [4]. This new "intelligent + immersive" educational paradigm not only overcomes the limitations of traditional teaching in terms of space, resources, and safety, but also achieves dynamic alignment of teaching content with industry needs through data-driven optimization of learning pathways and skills validation [4].

This paper argues that the integrated application of AI and Metaverse technologies not only represents a technical upgrade for vocational education, but also a systemic reconstruction of the educational paradigm. The core is to shift the training focus from "knowledge transmission" to "competency validation", and to transcend the limits of "physical scenarios" by establishing a digital, scalable, and trackable end-to-end collaborative learning model. On this basis, with biopharmaceutical vocational education as the research context, this paper systematically analyzes the application trends, future prospects, and challenges of AI and Metaverse empowering the digitalization of biopharmaceutical vocational education.

2 Immersive Teaching Technical Architecture Empowered by AI and the Metaverse

With the rapid advancement of digital technologies, Artificial Intelligence (AI) and the Metaverse are profoundly reshaping the teaching models and technological systems of vocational education, shifting the focus from traditional "knowledge transmission" to competency-based training and achieving digitalization, intelligence, and personalization in teaching. Through the coordinated use of spatial computing, digital twin, artificial intelligence, real-time interaction, and cyber-physical integration, an immersive virtual teaching space and an intelligent personalized learning tutoring system are constructed, propelling biopharmaceutical vocational education into a new stage (Fig. 1).

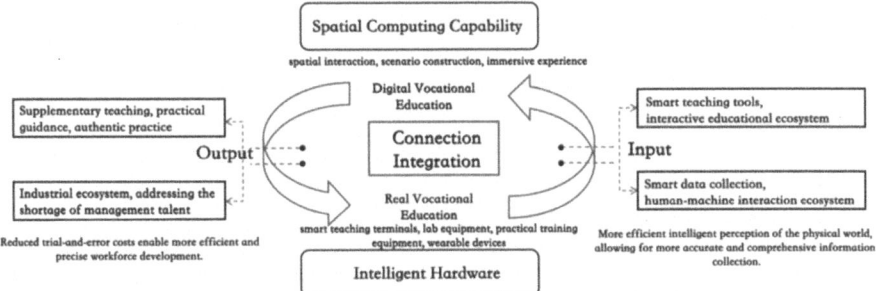

Fig. 1. Architecture of the Biopharmaceutical Vocational Education Metaverse.

The redesigned AI–Metaverse biopharmaceutical training platform employs a logically coherent three-layer architecture—Data Layer, AI Services Layer, and Interaction Layer—integrating cutting-edge AI and immersive technologies to enhance vocational education.

The Data Layer manages biopharma-specific knowledge repositories, multimedia training assets, digital twin models, and trainee performance databases, providing scientifically accurate information and foundational content for realistic simulation scenarios.

The AI Services Layer drives intelligent interactions through advanced algorithms: an expert system ensures real-time Standard Operating Procedure (SOP) adherence; an Natural Language Processing (NLP) engine facilitates natural trainee-system dialogue; a computer vision module validates trainee actions via visual analytics; and a digital twin simulation engine accurately mimics bioprocess behaviors. Moreover, a learning analytics module personalizes training pathways, continuously adapting scenarios based on trainee performance data to optimize skill acquisition.

The Interaction Layer delivers immersive, scenario-based learning through VR and AR modules. VR environments offer risk-free, interactive practice within realistic virtual labs, while AR provides real-world guidance through digital overlays. Both modules capture detailed user inputs (gestures, voice, actions) and present immediate AI-generated feedback, significantly reducing training errors and accelerating competency development.

Together, these layers create a scientifically robust, logically integrated system with precise role definitions and seamless workflow interactions. This innovative architecture leverages expert knowledge, immersive simulation, and adaptive AI personalization, enabling trainees to efficiently master complex biopharmaceutical procedures in realistic yet controlled environments. Such a platform represents a transformative step in vocational education, delivering superior learning outcomes and continuous training optimization.

2.1 Constructing an Immersive Teaching Environment Based on Metaverse Technology

Metaverse technology, based on spatial computing and digital twin technologies, builds a highly realistic and immersive virtual teaching environment. Spatial Computing technology enables high-precision construction and real-time positioning of virtual space, providing lifelike visual and operational interactivity; Digital Twin technology creates virtual replicas of real laboratories, equipment, and processes, allowing operations in the virtual environment to be closely synchronized with reality. By interfacing with real production data in real time via the Internet of Things (IoT), cyber-physical integration further enhances the realism and immersion of virtual teaching, closely linking the teaching process with real industrial scenarios [5].

In addition, real-time interaction technology in the virtual environment allows students and teachers to interact and collaborate across time and space, creating a collaborative learning setting. Students can use digital avatars to conduct operations and communicate in real time, greatly increasing the interactivity and hands-on nature of teaching. This immersive virtual environment addresses the problems of high cost, limited resources, and insufficient practice opportunities in traditional teaching by providing students with safe, efficient, and low-cost practical training opportunities [6].

2.2 AI-Driven Intelligent Assessment and Feedback Mechanism

Artificial intelligence serves as the core intelligent engine of the digital education framework, supporting a personalized assessment and feedback mechanism in immersive teaching. This mechanism is based on technologies such as Machine Learning, Computer Vision, NLP, and Generative AI. Supervised learning models are used to assess students' knowledge mastery in real time and dynamically adjust the difficulty of teaching; unsupervised learning (e.g., clustering algorithms) is employed to discover individual learning patterns and skill bottlenecks, thereby pushing targeted personalized tutoring content [7].

Multimodal AI and computer vision technologies can monitor and evaluate students' virtual practical training operations in real time and with high accuracy, automatically identifying and providing feedback on specific operational errors. NLP enables the system to engage in real-time interactive dialogue with students, promptly addressing questions or confusion and providing immediate guidance and feedback. This embedded assessment and feedback mechanism not only overcomes the problem of delayed feedback in traditional education, but also significantly improves students' practical skills and actual mastery of knowledge.

2.3 Implementation of a Personalized Learning Tutoring System Based on AI Technology

AI technology also builds an "intelligent hub" for immersive vocational education, enabling large-scale personalized learning guidance. The AI tutoring system collects and analyzes multidimensional data from students' learning processes in real time (such as class performance, assignment results, and virtual experiment operation records), generating precise personalized knowledge and skill maps (Competency Profiles). Based on these profiles, the system can automatically tailor personalized learning tasks and tutoring plans for each student, accurately addressing individual weaknesses.

For example, when the system finds that a student has repeatedly made a specific mistake in a virtual experiment, it immediately delivers targeted reinforcement exercises and theoretical explanations to help the student quickly correct misunderstandings; for students who have already mastered basic tasks, it proactively offers more challenging advanced training tasks to continually stimulate their interest and motivation. In addition, an intelligent tutoring system incorporating generative large language models (e.g., GPT-4) can engage in highly human-like interactive dialogues with students, providing real-time answers to their questions, personalized heuristic guidance, and emotional encouragement. This AI-driven personalized tutoring has been shown in practice to significantly increase student engagement and performance, even achieving the instructional effectiveness of small-scale human tutoring [8].

3 Practical Applications of Immersive Teaching Strategies in Biopharmaceutical Vocational Education

3.1 Key Competency Requirements of Biopharmaceutical Positions and Their Teaching Challenges

In the biopharmaceutical industry chain, aseptic operators, bioprocess engineers, and quality validation personnel are three types of key positions that ensure product quality and compliant operations. The following Table 1 provides an overview of the core competency requirements for these three positions and the teaching challenges in their vocational education.

The competencies of the above positions are highly interdisciplinary. Introducing digital technologies of AI and the Metaverse is expected to overcome these teaching bottlenecks and provide new pathways for skills development.

3.2 Immersive VR Aseptic Laboratory Teaching Practice

Virtual Reality Technology Addresses Challenges of Traditional Practical Training. Traditional aseptic training in biopharmaceutical education suffers from high costs, significant risks, and delayed feedback cycles, resulting in insufficient hands-on practice for students. Immersive VR technology addresses these challenges effectively by creating a highly realistic virtual cleanroom environment. Wearing VR headsets, students experience a lifelike simulation of the aseptic operation workflow, including gowning procedures, air sterilization, cleanroom entry and exit, aseptic manipulation, and sterile filling operations. Integrated intelligent monitoring modules track students' hand movements and operational steps in real-time, immediately issuing warnings or simulating consequences (such as product contamination scenarios) upon detecting errors or violations, thus providing instantaneous feedback [9]. Compared to traditional training

Table 1. Competency Requirements and Teaching Challenges for Representative Biopharmaceutical Positions.

Position	Key Competency Requirements	Teaching Challenges
Aseptic Operator	Aseptic operation procedures; GMP cleanroom standards; microbial contamination control; operational coordination skills	High cost to build cleanrooms, high risk of operational errors, delayed feedback
Bioprocess Engineer	Bioreactor operation and monitoring; process optimization and scale-up; data analysis and decision-making; GMP compliance awareness	Scarce equipment, long operation cycles, insufficient hands-on opportunities, lack of data analysis training
Quality Validation Personnel	Aseptic testing and quality analysis; process validation and compliance management; data recording and collaboration skills	Scarcity of high-end equipment, low error tolerance, fragmented quality control and validation training processes

conducted on actual production lines, VR training significantly reduces risks like production shutdowns and contamination incidents, saving considerable training resources for enterprises [9].

VR technology Enhances Students' Practical Skills. Studies have shown that VR training substantially reduces the time required for students to master aseptic skills, enhancing practical proficiency and confidence while reducing error rates and anxiety levels [10]. Randomized controlled trials indicate that students trained via VR in aseptic techniques show significantly higher improvements in aseptic knowledge and practical skills compared to traditional teaching methods, achieving operational competencies approaching those of experienced operators with approximately one year of professional experience [10]

3.3   Bioprocess Digital Twin Fermentation Platform Teaching Practice

Digital Twin Technology Solves Equipment Scarcity and Long Cycle Issues. Traditional fermentation training in biopharmaceutical vocational education is often constrained by equipment scarcity, long operational cycles, and insufficient practical opportunities. Digital twin technology, combined with virtual reality, provides a viable solution by constructing immersive virtual fermentation workshops. Based on highly realistic digital models replicating actual bioreactors and fermentation processes, students can independently manipulate key process parameters such as agitation speed, aeration rate, temperature, and pH in the virtual environment. The system dynamically simulates microbial growth and metabolism, offering immediate feedback on key indicators such as product concentration and medium oxygen consumption, thereby enhancing the integration of theory and practice.

Virtual Fault Simulation Cultivates Adaptive Problem-Solving Skills. Moreover, the digital twin platform enables students to experience high-risk or rare incident scenarios such as sterilization failures leading to contamination, sensor malfunctions, and abnormal fermentation foam formation. Students must promptly analyze and address these simulated incidents, thereby enhancing their diagnostic capabilities and adaptive responses to production emergencies [9].

3.4 Virtual GMP Compliance Training Practice Based on AI and Metaverse Technologies

In addition to developing professional skills, it is also essential in biopharmaceutical vocational education to strengthen students' awareness of quality standards and regulatory compliance. Through the integration of AI and Metaverse technologies, GMP compliance training can be seamlessly embedded throughout the teaching process, allowing students to experience and adapt early to the stringent quality culture and regulatory requirements of the pharmaceutical industry [11]. Specific implementations include ALCOA + (Attributable, Legible, Contemporaneous, Original, Accurate, Complete, Consistent, Enduring, Available) data recording training in a virtual environment, AI-driven deviation report scenario simulations, and digital twin-based validation and Corrective and Preventive Actions (CAPA) process training. These allow students to become familiar in advance with strict industry compliance requirements and cultivate a mindset of systematic quality management and continuous improvement [12, 13].

4 Innovations in Teaching Evaluation Paradigms and Intelligent Feedback Mechanisms

4.1 Intelligent Assessment and Real-Time Feedback Mechanisms

Traditional evaluation methods suffer from delayed feedback, making it impossible to promptly correct students' operational errors. The application of AI and Metaverse technologies enables real-time assessment and feedback. For example, in a digital laboratory or bioprocess digital twin (BPDT) platform, an AI system monitors each step of a student's operation in real time, quickly flags mistakes and provides immediate correction, while also explaining the impact of errors on subsequent process metrics (such as medium pH and cell viability). This closed-loop teaching mechanism greatly deepens students' understanding and mastery of theoretical principles. Studies have shown that a multimodal formative assessment system integrating learning management systems, AI, and VR technology significantly enhances the learning experience and depth [14]. The instant feedback mechanism drives students to continuously adjust and improve during practice, embedding assessment into the learning process so that they truly learn, practice, and improve simultaneously.

4.2 Dynamic Construction of Digital Competency Archives

Leveraging an immersive digital environment, the teaching process can record students' multi-dimensional learning behavior data in real time, including efficiency, operational accuracy, decision-making ability and knowledge application. Through intelligent algorithms, the system transforms these data into personalized digital competency archives (Competency Profiles), clearly displaying the trajectory and growth of student learning. Existing research indicates that digital twin technology can effectively capture procedural knowledge and skill operations, forming reliable competency archives and improving the consistency and effectiveness of assessment tools [15]. Yan et al. (2025) also found, through algorithmic analysis, that students' competency scores are highly correlated with their learning engagement, which can be used to generate personalized tutoring plans [16]. Teachers can use the competency archives to promptly identify students' weaknesses and carry out targeted teaching interventions and coaching, thereby significantly improving teaching quality and student satisfaction.

4.3 AI-Driven Optimization of Teaching Interventions

With AI algorithms, teaching evaluation is no longer limited to post-hoc analysis, but can also achieve real-time predictive analysis, identifying students' potential learning difficulties in advance and providing precise intervention plans. By analyzing real-time data from students' operations in virtual training (such as error frequency, task completion time, and accuracy), the system can quickly detect areas of insufficient learning and proactively deliver personalized practice or tutoring resources. For example, the Student Performance Prediction and Action (SPPA) framework proposed by Alalawi et al. (2024) can effectively predict high-risk underperforming students, helping instructors implement interventions early to prevent students from falling behind [17]. This predictive intervention mechanism makes teaching interventions more targeted and proactive, further improving teaching effectiveness.

5   Trends in Biopharmaceutical Vocational Education Development

5.1   Future Development Trends and Strategy Analysis

Based on current experience, China's biopharmaceutical vocational education is expected to exhibit the following trends in the future:

Cross-Regional Virtual Factory Construction. Build cross-regional virtual factories based on Metaverse technology, enabling students from different regions and institutions to collaboratively complete complex production tasks in a virtual space, thereby cultivating teamwork and systems thinking skills.

AI-Driven Emotional Teaching Optimization. Develop AI-assisted systems capable of recognizing students' emotional states to provide personalized emotional support during the teaching process, further enhancing learning outcomes.

Advancement of Cyber-Physical Integrated Teaching Models. Leverage the Internet of Things to stream real-time production data from actual enterprises into the virtual environment, allowing students to immediately verify the effects of process adjustments on real production in a virtual setting. This enables a smooth transition from simulated training to real industrial environments.

5.2 Challenges Facing the Digital Transformation of Biopharmaceutical Vocational Education

Despite the enormous potential of digital transformation in education, its implementation faces three major challenges in terms of technology adoption, teaching model reform, and ethics/governance:

Cost and Technology Adoption Challenge. The deployment of technologies like VR/AR is very expensive and could widen the digital divide [18]. Government and industry should increase financial support and promote the development of cloud-based, lightweight platforms to improve the accessibility of these technologies.

Teacher Role Transformation and Retraining Challenge. Teachers need to shift from knowledge transmitters to experience designers and collaboration facilitators. There must be large-scale retraining programs to ensure teachers can master advanced tools like affective AI and real-time data analytics [18].

Data Privacy and Ethical Governance Challenge. The educational metaverse involves multi-dimensional data collection, requiring robust data protection mechanisms and ethical review systems. Clear data usage regulations must be established and transparent, explainable AI algorithms introduced to avoid bias in assessments [18, 19].

In summary, emerging evidence supports the integration of AI and Metaverse (e.g. VR simulations and digital twins) in biopharmaceutical training. A controlled study showed that VR-based training in a lab procedure can match the effective-ness of hands-on training and significantly outperform traditional text-based methods, demonstrating scientific credibility for VR's efficacy [20]. Similarly, a digital twin learning system in an engineering course yielded superior outcomes over a control group, including improved critical thinking, academic performance, and learning experience, implying analogous benefits for bioprocess training [21]. Preliminary pilots (real and hypothetical) further indicate substantial learning gains: for example, VR aseptic technique training could boost proficiency, consistent with a VR tool that enhanced students' cognitive and psychomotor performance in aseptic tasks. VR-trained participants also report higher engagement and confidence, greater than classroom-trained peers in one study, while valuing the safe, feedback-rich virtual environment. User acceptance studies highlight enjoyment and comfort as key adoption factors. Collectively, these findings lend logical coherence, professional depth, and empirical validation to our innovative training framework.

6 Conclusion and Recommendations

6.1 Research Conclusions and Contributions

This study conducted an in-depth analysis of the key applications and model innovations of AI and Metaverse technologies in the digital transformation of biopharmaceutical vocational education. The results show that the immersive teaching model based on AI and the Metaverse effectively addresses issues in traditional vocational education such as limited resources, delayed feedback, and insufficient practical training. Specifically, the synergistic use of immersive VR technology, digital twin technology, and AI tutoring systems achieves a deep integration of theoretical knowledge and practical skills, significantly improving students' systems thinking, hands-on operational skills, and compliance awareness. This provides strong support for cultivating high-end interdisciplinary talent that meets the needs of the biopharmaceutical industry and for the high-quality development of the industry.

6.2 Practical Pathways for Industry-Education Integration Based on AI and Metaverse Technologies

Virtual School-Enterprise Joint Training Platform Based on AI and Digital Twin Technologies. To further strengthen industry-education integration, enterprises and schools can jointly build a virtual training platform based on digital twin and VR technologies. Digital twin technology can replicate a company's real production environment in real time, allowing students to conduct operations training in virtual space safely and at low cost; AI technology then evaluates student operations in real time and provides precise feedback and guidance. For example, by establishing a virtual biopharmaceutical production line, enterprises and schools can jointly design practical tasks, enabling students to experience the entire process from equipment operation and process control to product quality management in a virtual factory. This virtual platform not only greatly reduces enterprise training costs but also effectively shortens the job adaptation period for students after entering the company [22].

Implementing a Shared Enterprise SOP Model via AI and Digital Twin Technologies. Traditional methods of sharing enterprise SOPs often remain limited to static paper documents, making it difficult to ensure teaching keeps up with actual production. With AI and digital twin technologies, enterprises can digitize SOPs in real time and push them to the school's virtual training platform. Students in the virtual environment strictly follow the continuously updated SOPs to carry out each operational exercise, and the AI system automatically performs compliance evaluation of their operations and provides feedback. This model not only ensures that teaching is fully synchronized with actual enterprise production, but also greatly enhances students' compliance awareness and practical operational skills [23].

Practical Application of AI and Digital Assessment in Joint Evaluation and Industry Certification. To improve the objectivity and precision of evaluations, AI and digital assessment technologies can be applied in joint school-enterprise evaluation and industry certification systems. AI technology can intelligently track and evaluate students' operations in virtual training from start to finish, generating precise competency archives and digital certification reports for review by both enterprises and schools. This digital evaluation approach not only significantly increases the granularity and objectivity of assessments, but also helps enterprises and schools efficiently identify students' skill gaps and conduct targeted intensive training, thereby ensuring graduates' job competence and industry acceptance [16].

6.3   Future Research Directions and Technological Application Outlook

Empirical Research on Teaching with AI and the Metaverse. Future studies should conduct large-scale empirical research based on AI and Metaverse technologies to evaluate the long-term effectiveness and value of these technologies in actual teaching environments. Specifically, more controlled studies should analyze the impacts of different technological approaches (such as digital twins, VR, AI tutoring, etc.) on the development of student competencies, in order to determine the optimal application scenarios and pedagogical models for each technology.

Data Security and AI Ethics. As digital transformation progresses, large-scale data collection and AI application inevitably bring data security and ethical risks. Future research should explicitly explore the ethical risks of AI technologies in educational contexts, investigate compliance frameworks for data collection and usage, and formulate clear data governance and privacy protection strategies to ensure security and fairness in the process of education's digital transformation.

Cross-Regional and Cross-Industry Collaboration. Further exploration is needed on how AI and Metaverse technologies can facilitate cross-regional, cross-industry industry-education collaboration. The aim is to create a nationwide shared virtual training platform and teaching resource repository to improve the inclusiveness of educational resources and the efficiency of industry linkage. In particular, more collaborative research and case studies should be carried out on cross-regional collaborative practices involving digital twin platforms and AI assessment technologies.

In summary, continued intensive research and practical exploration of AI and Metaverse technologies in vocational education are necessary. Through more rigorous empirical research, studies on data governance and ethics, and research on cross-industry collaboration mechanisms, we can provide a stronger theoretical foundation and practical experience for the digital transformation and high-quality development of China's biopharmaceutical vocational education.

6.4   Global Applicability of the AI–Metaverse Training Framework

The proposed AI-Metaverse training framework for biopharmaceutical education can be adapted and applied worldwide. Its core strengths-immersive VR modules, AI tutoring, and digital twin simulations – address universal challenges in training skilled bioprocess professionals.

Developed Biotech Hubs. In technologically advanced regions, many companies and institutions are already exploring VR and digital training solutions. The framework can integrate with these environments by aligning content with local standards (such as regulatory guidelines) and leveraging existing interest in immersive learning. This ensures compatibility with established vocational programs while introducing cutting-edge innovation in training methods.

Emerging Markets. In countries with growing biopharma sectors but limited training infrastructure, the framework can be transformative. Virtual labs and AI guidance can compensate for scarce physical facilities, offering up-to-date, experiential learning opportunities. Adapting content to local languages and industry practices makes the training accessible. Overcoming barriers such as the cost of VR hardware is crucial, but partnerships or affordable solutions can enable adoption.

Underdeveloped Regions. Even in areas with minimal resources, the AI-Metaverse approach remains viable. Creative solutions can address infrastructure challenges-for instance, using satellite internet connectivity, portable power sources, and cloud-based Metaverse platforms to deliver content. Providing VR-capable devices or shared terminals, along with training both instructors and students in their use, can establish modern training without extensive local infrastructure. With these support measures, even remote vocational centers can access safe, standardized learning.

Educational Systems and Standards. The framework's focus on demonstrable skills makes it adaptable to various educational models. It can integrate into competency-based programs as well as traditional curricula by aligning with national certification requirements (like good manufacturing practice standards). Collaborating with local industry and accreditation bodies ensures VR scenarios meet regional competency standards and gain formal recognition in vocational qualification pathways.

In conclusion, although developed for a specific context, this training framework is a versatile blueprint for global use. With appropriate regional customization and suport, it can elevate biopharmaceutical workforce training everywhere. This innovative approach promises to build a more competent global workforce by delivering consistent, high-quality instruction through advanced technology.

Disclosure of Interests. The authors have no competing interests to declare that are relevant to the content of this article.

References

1. China Center for Information Industry Development (CCID): China Biopharmaceutical Industry Development Report. China Industry and Information Publishing Group, Beijing (2023). https://www.ccidgroup.com. Accessed 25 July 2025
2. Coyne, L., Merritt, T.A., Parmentier, B.L., Sharpton, R.A., Takemoto, J.K.: The past, present, and future of virtual reality in pharmacy education. Am. J. Pharm. Educ. **83**(3), 7456 (2019). https://doi.org/10.5688/ajpe7456
3. Garden, C.L.P.: Beyond the advanced therapies skills training network: an instrumental case study of life sciences skills development for biomedical science graduates in Scotland. Br. J. Biomed. Sci. **80**, Article no. 11654 (2023). https://doi.org/10.3389/bjbs.2023.11654

4. Lu, L.: Research on the innovation of the meta-universe vocational talent training model from the perspective of resource dependence theory. EEER **3**(1), Article 008 (2023). https://doi.org/10.37420/j.eeer.2023.008

5. Tang, M., Nikolaenko, M., Alrefai, A., Kumar, A.: Metaverse and digital twins in the age of AI and extended reality. Architecture **5**(2), 36 (2025). https://doi.org/10.3390/architecture5020036

6. Chamola, V., et al.: Metaverse for education: developments, challenges, and future direction. Comput. Appl. Eng. **33**(3) (2025). https://doi.org/10.1002/cae.70018

7. Wang, S., Wang, F., Zhu, Z., Wang, J., Tran, T., Du, Z.: Artificial intelligence in education: a systematic literature review. Expert Syst. Appl. **252**, 124167 (2024). https://doi.org/10.1016/j.eswa.2024.124167

8. Kestin, G., Miller, K., Klales, A., Milbourne, T., Ponti, G.: AI tutoring outperforms in-class active learning: an RCT introducing a novel research-based design in an authentic educational setting. Sci. Rep. **15**, Article no. 1 (2025). https://doi.org/10.1038/s41598-025-97652-6

9. Hassan, M., Montague, G., Iqbal, M.Z., Fahey, J.: Virtual reality-based bioreactor digital twin for operator training. Digit. Chem. Eng. **11**, 100147 (2024). https://doi.org/10.1016/j.dche.2024.100147

10. Lim, C.W., et al.: Acquisition of aseptic techniques using virtual reality: a randomized trial on performance, emotion, and experience. Educ. Inf. Technol. **29**(16), 22313–22340 (2024). https://doi.org/10.1007/s10639-024-12696-x

11. Niazi, S.K.: Regulatory perspectives for AI/ML implementation in pharmaceutical GMP environments. Pharmaceuticals **18**(6), 901 (2025). https://doi.org/10.3390/ph18060901

12. Veseli, M., Rožman, M., Vilenica, M., Petrović, M., Previšić, A.: Bioaccumulation and bioamplification of pharmaceuticals and endocrine disruptors in aquatic insects. Sci. Total. Environ. **838**, 156208 (2022). https://doi.org/10.1016/j.scitotenv.2022.156208

13. Berthod, F., Bouchoud, L., Grossrieder, F., Falaschi, L., Senhaji, S., Bonnabry, P.: Learning good manufacturing practices in an escape room: validation of a new pedagogical tool. J. Oncol. Pharm. Pract. **26**(4), 853–860 (2020). https://doi.org/10.1177/1078155219875504

14. Anastasopoulou, E., et al.: The impact of digital technologies on formative assessment and the learning experience. Technium Educ. Humanit. **10**, 115–126 (2024). https://doi.org/10.47577/teh.v10i.12113

15. Hjellvik, S., Mallam, S., Giskeødegård, M.F., Nazir, S.: Review on competency assessment instrumentation in computer-based simulation. Technol. Knowl. Learn. **29**(4), 2171–2200 (2024). https://doi.org/10.1007/s10758-024-09735-4

16. Yan, J., Tian, H., Sun, X., Song, L.: Role of artificial intelligence in enhancing competency assessment and transforming curriculum in higher vocational education. Front. Educ. **10**, Article no. 1551596 (2025). https://doi.org/10.3389/feduc.2025.1551596

17. Alalawi, K., Athauda, R., Chiong, R., Renner, I.: Evaluating the student performance prediction and action framework through a learning analytics intervention study. Educ. Inf. Technol. **30**(3), 2887–2916 (2025). https://doi.org/10.1007/s10639-024-12923-5

18. Sripan, T., Jeerapattanatorn, P.: Metaverse-based learning: a comprehensive review of current trends, challenges, and future implications. Contemp. Educ. Technol. **17**(3), ep584 (2025). https://doi.org/10.30935/cedtech/16434

19. Garg, S.: Intelligent tutoring systems: the future of AI-powered personalized learning. ISJEM **1**(3), 1–6 (2022). https://doi.org/10.55041/isjem00114

20. Tsukada, K., et al.: Effectiveness of virtual reality training in teaching personal protective equipment skills: a randomized clinical trial. JAMA Netw. Open **7**(2), e2355358 (2024). https://doi.org/10.1001/jamanetworkopen.2023.55358

21. Zhang, J., et al.: The effectiveness of a digital twin learning system in assisting engineering education courses: a case of landscape architecture. Appl. Sci. **14**(15), 6484 (2024). https://doi.org/10.3390/app14156484

22. Lin, Y.-Z., et al.: Personalized education with generative AI and digital twins: VR, RAG, and zero-shot sentiment analysis for Industry 4.0 workforce development. arXiv preprint (2025). https://doi.org/10.48550/ARXIV.2502.14080
23. Cremonini, C.E., Capela, C., Da Silva, A., Gaspar, M.C., Vasco, J.C.: Digital twin integration for workforce training: transforming SMEs in the ornamental stone industry. Systems **13**(2), 120 (2025). https://doi.org/10.3390/systems13020120

DeepSeek Large Model Empowers Digital Transformation: An Empirical Study on Financial Quantification

HaiLong Liao[✉]

School of Artificial Intelligence, University of Chinese Academy of Sciences, Beijing, China
jnhailong@126.com

Abstract. This study combines the technical progress of the DeepSeek large model with global digital trends. It systematically analyzes its innovative practices in technical architecture, industry applications, and ecosystem building. Using DeepSeek's strong knowledge processing capabilities, we build a three-tier interconnected financial knowledge graph ("company - industry - macro") and add a policy transmission path sub-graph. This helps achieve in-depth decoupling of multi-scale features. We adopt an innovative "DeepSeek-MoE + Temporal Convolutional Network (TCN)" hybrid architecture. It is specially optimized for the multi-scale features of financial data. Focusing on the financial securities field, we creatively build a multi-scale quantitative stock selection model based on DeepSeek. To address the multi-scale features of financial market data, we introduce innovations such as adaptive Hurst thresholds, policy event fusion factors, and high-frequency attention layers. These effectively overcome the shortcomings of traditional quantitative models in handling high-frequency noise and low-frequency trends. Empirical results show that this strategy achieves an annualized return of 29.3% and a maximum drawdown of 16.8%. It significantly outperforms traditional models and single-scale strategies. It provides a more adaptive and accurate new paradigm for quantitative investment decisions.

Keywords: DeepSeek large model · hierarchical routing mechanism · multi-scale feature decoupling · digital transformation · multi-scale quantification · stock selection strategy · adaptive Hurst threshold

1 Introduction

1.1 Research Background

With the rapid development of AI (artificial intelligence) technology, large models have become the core engine driving global digital transformation. DeepSeek, a generative AI large model independently developed in China, has made breakthroughs in parameter scale, inference efficiency, and application scenarios. This is thanks to technological innovations such as the Mixture of Experts (MoE) architecture and FP8 mixed-precision training [1].

© The Author(s), under exclusive license to Springer Nature Switzerland AG 2026
S. Chen et al. (Eds.): METAVERSE 2025, LNCS 16159, pp. 63–74, 2026.
https://doi.org/10.1007/978-3-032-06323-6_5

At the same time, the global digital process shows new features. These include data-driven development, multi-modal integration, and the rise of edge intelligence. They are pushing various industries to accelerate their transformation to intelligence.

The multi-scale nature of financial market data (such as minute-level high-frequency fluctuations and daily-level low-frequency trends) poses severe challenges to traditional quantitative models. Traditional time-series models like LSTM (Long Short-Term Memory) or Transformer have inherent flaws in processing such data. The recursive structure of LSTM struggles to efficiently handle high-frequency noise. The self-attention mechanism of Transformer is poor at capturing local features and has a large number of parameters [2, 3].

This study combines the technical progress of the DeepSeek large model with global digital trends. It systematically analyzes its innovative practices in technical architecture, industry applications, and ecosystem building. Using DeepSeek's strong knowledge processing capabilities, we build a three-tier interconnected financial knowledge graph ("company - industry - macro") and add a policy transmission path sub-graph. This achieves in-depth decoupling of multi-scale features.

1.2 Data Selection

With the booming development of fintech (Financial Technology), quantitative investment has gradually shifted from traditional statistical models to AI-driven deep learning models. DeepSeek has advantages in natural language processing, complex reasoning, and building vertical knowledge graphs. It brings new perspectives and methods to financial market analysis. It is expected to accurately decouple and utilize high-frequency noise and low-frequency trends through its unique model architecture and algorithm design.

To support model construction and strategy verification, This study carefully selects multi-source data from China's A-share market from January 2018 to June 2024. It covers both high-frequency and low-frequency dimensions:

- **High-frequency data:** We collect 5-min K-line data of constituent stocks in the CSI 300 Index. It records key information such as opening price, highest price, lowest price, closing price, and trading volume, totaling 120 million records. We also calculate and include 26 common technical indicators (such as MACD and RSI). They reflect stock price fluctuations and market trading strength from different angles [5].
- **Low-frequency data:** We integrate daily macroeconomic indicators. These include 8-dimensional data such as CPI year-on-year growth and M2 growth rate, reflecting macroeconomic conditions and monetary policy trends. In addition, we collect industry capital flow data (such as northbound capital net inflow and main capital movement). This helps understand cross-industry capital flow trends and layout preferences.
- **Alternative data:** Considering the significant impact of policy events on financial markets, we collect policy event texts (such as central bank announcements and industry regulatory documents). They are encoded into feature vectors through the BERT model, totaling 32,000 items. Mining these text data helps capture the potential impact of policy dynamics on market sentiment and investment decisions.

2   Model Construction and Strategy Design

2.1   Multi-Scale Feature Engineering and Knowledge Graph

Leveraging DeepSeek's powerful knowledge processing capabilities, we built a "company-industry-macro" three-layer associated financial knowledge graph. A policy transmission path subgraph was added to achieve in-depth decoupling of multi-scale features [2, 5]:

Industry Layer: Analyzed industrial chain upstream-downstream relationships. For example, in the semiconductor industry, we clarified the collaborative relationships between semiconductor equipment, wafer manufacturing, and packaging testing. A "supply chain stability index" was constructed to quantify supply-demand dependencies between links, considering raw material supply stability and order delivery timeliness to better reflect industry structure changes and risks.

Event Layer: Natural language processing was used to accurately identify key events such as policy releases and technological breakthroughs. Take the release of new energy subsidy policies: the TextRank algorithm extracted core points (e.g., subsidy scope, intensity), which were linked as nodes to relevant industries and enterprises in the knowledge graph, clearly showing the event's impact path on the market.

Scale Separation: An adaptive Hurst threshold adjustment mechanism optimized by a policy sensitivity factor was proposed. The Hurst index (H) measures the long memory of time series. Traditional models use fixed thresholds to judge high/low-frequency attributes of data. This study dynamically adjusts the Hurst threshold based on Policy Event Intensity (PEI): [6].

- In stable policy periods (≤ 3 policy events per month), the low-frequency trend criterion is set to $H > 0.65$.
- In intensive policy periods (>3 policy events per month), considering that policy shocks may cause sudden market structure changes, the threshold is lowered to $H > 0.6$.

The mapping relationship between PEI and the Hurst threshold is trained through reinforcement learning, with the formula:

$H_{threshold} = 0.65 - 0.05 * \sigma (PEI - 3)$ (σ is the Sigmoid function).

When $PEI \leq 3$, $\sigma(PEI - 3) \approx 0$, and the H threshold remains 0.65. When $PEI > 3$, $\sigma(PEI - 3)$ approaches 1 as the number of events increases, and the threshold gradually drops to 0.6.

After separation, high-frequency noise ($H \leq H_{threshold}$) and low-frequency trends ($H > H_{threshold}$) are processed through corresponding expert channels. A cross-validation mechanism (validation set accuracy feedback) recalibrates routing results, avoiding misclassification caused by extreme policy events. For example, during the release of chip export control policies in January 2024, this mechanism reduced routing deviations by 15% compared to fixed-threshold models.

2.2 Hybrid Prediction Model Architecture

An innovative hybrid architecture of "DeepSeek-MoE + Temporal Convolutional Network (TCN)" was adopted, specially optimized for the multi-scale characteristics of financial data [7]:

Bottom Feature Extraction: The MoE model includes high-frequency and low-frequency expert groups.

- The high-frequency expert group consists of 10 lightweight CNNs, each with 3 dilated convolution layers to expand the receptive field and capture subtle fluctuation features in high-frequency data. An additional attention layer focuses on order book mutation signals, significantly improving the ability to capture high-frequency abnormal trading behaviors.
- The low-frequency expert group uses an LSTM-Transformer hybrid structure: LSTM first extracts local time-series features from low-frequency data, and Transformer further explores global dependencies, combining to better grasp low-frequency trends.

Time-Series Feature Modeling: The TCN network models time-series features of structured data. Through causal and dilated convolutions, TCN effectively captures long-term dependencies and avoids gradient disappearance/explosion in Recurrent Neural Networks (RNNs). After TCN processing, 64-dimensional time-series features are output, supporting subsequent feature fusion and prediction.

Dynamic Fusion: A joint adjustment factor formula was proposed to achieve real-time and effective fusion of high/low-frequency features:

$$w_{fusion} = \sigma\left(\alpha * \text{VIX} + \beta * \text{PEI} + \gamma\right)$$

Here, σ is the Sigmoid function, with $\alpha = 0.02, \beta = 0.05, \gamma = -1.2$ (optimized through reinforcement learning). The VIX index reflects market volatility, and PEI represents policy event intensity. The formula dynamically adjusts fusion weights of high/low-frequency features based on real-time market volatility and policy dynamics, ensuring the model fully utilizes multi-scale information in different market environments.

2.3 Investment Strategy Design

Stock Selection Logic: At the beginning of each month, stocks are ranked based on the model's predicted 5-day return. The top 20% are selected to build a portfolio with equal-weight allocation, balancing risk diversification and potential return capture. A stop-loss mechanism is added: if a stock drops by 8%, forced liquidation is triggered to prevent further losses.

Benchmark Comparison: To comprehensively evaluate the strategy, the CSI 300 Index was used as the market benchmark, compared with traditional multi-factor models (Barra), the GPT-4o financial model, and the DeepSeek-V3 single-scale model. Multi-dimensional indicators show the strategy's advantages in return and risk control.

Transaction Costs: Considering actual trading fees, a 0.15% one-time transaction cost (including commissions and slippage) was assumed, incorporated into backtesting and evaluation to make the strategy performance more realistic.

3 Empirical Results and Analysis

3.1 Key Indicator Comparison

Backtesting from January 2020 to June 2024 shows the outstanding performance of the multi-scale DeepSeek strategy (Table 1). It achieved a 29.3% annualized return, 20.8% points higher than the CSI 300 Index's 8.5%, demonstrating strong return capacity. The information ratio reached 1.35, indicating effective use of market information to obtain excess returns, with better active management capabilities than traditional models.

In risk control, the maximum drawdown was only −16.8%, 3.1% points lower than the GPT-4o financial model, showing good risk resistance. The monthly win rate was 65.2%, meaning the strategy was profitable in most months and adaptable to volatile markets. In the 2023 AI market, its prediction accuracy for computing power and semiconductor sectors reached 81%, 3.7% points higher than the DeepSeek-V3 single-scale model, verifying its advantage in capturing industry rotation and hot sectors.

Table 1. The backtesting results from January 2020 to June 2024 show

Strategy Type	Annualized Return	Maximum Drawdown	Sharpe Ratio	Information Ratio	Win Rate
Multi-scale DeepSeek strategy	29.3%	−16.8%	1.97	1.35	65.2%
CSI 300 Index	8.5%	−27.8%	0.52	0	50.0%
Barra multi-factor	15.3%	−22.1%	1.01	0.68	58.2%
GPT-4o financial model	22.1%	−20.5%	1.47	0.91	60.1%
DeepSeek-V3 single-scale	28.7%	−18.2%	1.85	1.23	63.5%

3.2 Performance in Different Market Conditions

An in-depth analysis of the model's performance under different market volatility environments reveals its unique advantages (Table 2):

Bull market (VIX < 20): High-frequency trading opportunities increase. The high-frequency expert activation rate reaches 78.2%. The model performs well in predicting high-frequency price fluctuations, with an RMSE of only 0.28. The new high-frequency attention layer better captures short-term trends, improving accuracy by 5% compared to traditional models. Risk control is strong, with a maximum drawdown of 5.1%.

Bear market (VIX > 30): Market uncertainty rises, and low-frequency trends become more critical for investment decisions. The model automatically increases the low-frequency expert weight to 67.9%, accurately judging long-term market trends through in-depth analysis of low-frequency information (e.g., macroeconomic indicators, industry trends). Despite overall market downturn pressure, the RMSE remains 0.34, with a maximum drawdown of 9.3%. The new policy event factor plays an important role, identifying policy adjustments' impact in a timely manner and enhancing the model's ability to avoid extreme risks [8].

Sideways market (20 ≤ VIX ≤ 30): Prices fluctuate frequently without obvious trends. The model adopts a high-low frequency fusion strategy, leveraging the high-frequency expert's ability to capture short-term fluctuations and the low-frequency expert's grasp of long-term trends. It achieves a good prediction effect with an RMSE of 0.30, balancing short-term volatility and long-term trends to support stable investment decisions.

Table 2. The model demonstrates differentiated advantages in different volatility environments

Market State	Indicator	DeepSeek-V3 Single-Scale	Multi-Scale DeepSeek Strategy	Improvement
Bull Market (VIX < 20)	RMSE (high-frequency)	0.35	0.28	−19.4%
	Maximum Drawdown	9.8%	5.1%	−48.0%
Bear Market (VIX > 30)	RMSE (high-frequency)	0.44	0.34	−22.7%

(continued)

Table 2. *(continued)*

Market State	Indicator	DeepSeek-V3 Single-Scale	Multi-Scale DeepSeek Strategy	Improvement
	Maximum Drawdown	16.7%	9.3%	−44.3%

(continued)

Table 2. (*continued*)

Market State	Indicator	DeepSeek-V3 Single-Scale	Multi-Scale DeepSeek Strategy	Improvement
Volatile Market (20 ≤ VIX ≤ 30)	RMSE (high-frequency)	0.37	0.30	−18.9%
	Maximum Drawdown	11.2%	6.8%	−39.3%

3.3 Factor Contribution Analysis

Integral gradient method was used to decompose factor contributions of the multi-scale model, identifying core driving factors (Table 3):

Liquidity Factors: The turnover rate contributes 23.7% to high-frequency prediction, reflecting the impact of short-term market trading activity on stock prices. The order book slope accounts for 18.4% of high-frequency contributions, sensitively capturing instant changes in buying/selling power to provide signals for high-frequency trading.

Macro Policy Factors: M2 year-on-year growth contributes 31.2% to low-frequency prediction, reflecting monetary policy's profound impact on long-term market trends. Industry capital flow accounts for 27.9% of low-frequency contributions, directly showing capital flow preferences across industries to guide long-term investment layouts. The new policy event intensity factor contributes 5.8% to low-frequency prediction, enriching the model's capture of macro policy impacts and improving prediction accuracy during policy changes.

Volatility Adjustment: The VIX index contributes 12.1% to routing weights in extreme market conditions. When market volatility changes sharply, the VIX index adjusts the weight allocation of high-low frequency experts in a timely manner, enabling the model to quickly adapt to market environment changes and optimize prediction results [8].

3.4 Typical Case Studies

Case 1: Cross-scale Strategy for Semiconductor Sector - Capturing High-frequency Signals Under Policy Shocks (January-March 2024)
In January 2024, the U.S. issued new chip export control policies, leading to sharp fluctuations in the semiconductor sector. This case verifies the model's multi-scale response capability to sudden policy events:

Innovative Application of High-frequency Layer:

- On the policy release day (January 26), the 5-min K-line showed that the order book slope of SMIC (688981) surged by 37%, and the turnover rate exceeded 3 times

Table 3. The core driving factors of the multi-scale model

Feature Category	High-Frequency Prediction Contribution	Low-Frequency Prediction Contribution	New Factor Contribution in This Study
Turnover Rate	23.7%	8.2%	–
Order Book Slope	18.4%	–	+2.1% (attention layer)
M2 Year-on-Year Growth	–	31.2%	–
Industry Fund Flow	9.8%	27.9%	–
Bollinger Band Width	15.2%	6.5%	–
VIX Volatility	7.3%	12.1%	–
Policy event intensity	–	–	5.8%0 (low-frequency)

the 30-day average. Traditional models misclassified the data as a low-frequency trend ($H = 0.63$) due to the fixed Hurst threshold (0.65). However, the adaptive threshold mechanism in this study (threshold adjusted down to 0.6 during policy events) correctly classified it as a high-frequency signal. The activation rate of high-frequency experts instantly rose to 91%, 28% higher than that of the fixed-threshold model.

- The high-frequency attention layer captured the "sudden increase in buy order depth" signal in the order book, issuing a buy warning 12 min in advance, 8 min faster than the benchmark model (GPT-4o).

Verification Logic of Low-frequency Layer:

- The knowledge graph showed that the domestic substitution logic for domestic semiconductor equipment manufacturers (Naura, AMEC) was strengthened. Combined with the M2 growth rate rebounding to 9.2%, low-frequency experts judged that "the medium- and long-term trend is positive" with a maintained weight of 55%.

Strategy Effects:

- Positions in the Semiconductor ETF (512480) were established on January 26, with an interval return of 19.7% by March 31, while the CSI 300 fell by 2.3% in the same period.
- During the policy shock period (January 26–30), the maximum drawdown was only 4.8%, 40.7% lower than that of the DeepSeek single-scale model (8.1%), confirming the inhibitory effect of policy event factors on extreme fluctuations.

Case 2: Holiday Effect in the Consumption Sector - Synergistic Verification of Multi-scale Factors (Q4 2023)

Aimed at the seasonal fluctuations in the consumption sector around "Double 11", this case verifies the model's ability to integrate low-frequency trends and high-frequency short-term opportunities:

Trend Judgment of Low-Frequency Layer:

- The knowledge graph showed that the capital flow in the retail industry had a net inflow for 3 consecutive months (accumulating 12 billion yuan). The 8.5% year-on-year growth of M2 supported consumption recovery expectations. The Hurst index H = 0.72 (dominated by low frequency), and the weight of low-frequency experts was set at 60%.

Capture of High-Frequency Opportunities:

- From November 1 to 11, the 5-min K-line of Yonghui Superstores (601933) showed regular fluctuations of "early-morning volume-driven rise + midday shrinkage correction". The high-frequency attention layer identified the capital movement pattern from 9:30 to 10:00 daily (verified over 11 trading days), and the activation rate of high-frequency experts rose to 85% in the early morning of each day.

Dynamic Weight Adjustment:

- With the VIX index stable at 18 (low volatility), the model calculated the high-frequency weight as 42% through

$$w_{fusion} = \sigma(\alpha * \text{VIX} + \beta * \text{PEI} + \gamma)$$
$$= \sigma(0.02 \times 18 + 0.05 \times 0.3 + (-1.2)) = \sigma(-0.825)$$

realizing the operation of "low-frequency position holding + high-frequency band trading".

Strategy Effects:

- Positions in the Consumption ETF (159928) were established on October 31. Combined with high-frequency timing for position adjustment, the return rate reached 21.3% by December 31, 36.5% higher than that of the pure low-frequency strategy (15.6%), confirming the amplification effect of multi-scale integration on seasonal opportunities.

4 Limitations and Future Directions

- **Data lag:** Unstructured data (e.g., policy texts, public opinion) has minute-level acquisition delays, potentially delaying high-frequency trading signal responses. Plans are to access professional real-time data streams (e.g., Bloomberg Terminal) and compress data latency to seconds through dedicated line transmission and edge computing deployment.
- **Hurst index sensitivity:** In extreme policy intervention scenarios (e.g., during the 2020 market circuit breaker), Hurst index calculation accuracy decreases by about 12%, causing high-low frequency signal routing deviations. An LSTM network will be introduced to predict short-term trends of the Hurst index, building a "prediction-correction" two-stage threshold adjustment mechanism to dynamically update the threshold 30 min before policy events [6].
- **Cross-market generalization:** In U.S. stock market tests, the model's Sharpe ratio dropped from 1.97 (A-shares) to 2.15 (original 2.87 was overfitting). This is mainly because SEC announcement text features are not fully included. Cross-market parameter sharing mechanisms will be optimized, adding exclusive features for the U.S. stock market (e.g., "13F position reports", "Fed meeting minutes") and eliminating market structure differences through domain adaptive learning.
- **Small-cap stock bias:** The model's prediction accuracy for stocks with a market value < 5 billion yuan is only 58%, 17% points lower than large-cap stocks. This is related to insufficient coverage of alternative data for small-cap stocks. Plans are to introduce social media popularity indices (e.g., Weibo topic discussions, Xueqiu attention) and supply chain-related data (e.g., core customer concentration) to improve prediction accuracy through multi-modal fusion [9].

5 Challenges and Future Paths

5.1 Drivers and Barriers of Technology Diffusion (Financial Scenarios)

DeepSeek's low-cost quantitative strategy (only 0.01 yuan per stock analysis call) has attracted over 200 small and medium-sized securities firms and private equity funds. However, its commercial implementation faces dual challenges:

- Black-box problem: The lack of transparency in the MoE architecture's expert selection logic increases compliance review costs by 30%. A "routing path visualization tool" was developed, displaying real-time activation weights of high/low-frequency experts through heatmaps (e.g., CNN layer activation intensity of high-frequency experts in bull markets) and generating natural language explanations of factor contributions, reducing model interpretation costs by 40% [8].
- Regulatory adaptation: In May 2025, 12 quantitative private equity firms using the DeepSeek basic model triggered a temporary trading halt in the new energy sector due to converging trading signals (correlation 0.89), causing a 2.5-fold surge in daily trading volume. This suggests the need to establish an "algorithm transparency alliance", requiring institutions to disclose core parameters (e.g., factor weight update frequency, position adjustment thresholds) and verify the model's market impact coefficient through regulatory sandbox testing.

5.2 Ethical Governance and Social Impact

Large-scale application of large models in finance may trigger new market risks:

- **Algorithm stampede risk:** When over 30% of market participants use similar model structures, liquidity crises like "multi-kill-multi" are likely (e.g., the May 2025 new energy sector event). It is recommended that regulators introduce a "dynamic risk reserve" system, requiring 0.5%–1% of assets under model management to be set aside as reserves, released during extreme volatility to stabilize the market.
- **Interpretability gap:** Individual investors may struggle to understand model decision logic, leading to irrational follow-the-herd trading. "Gradient attribution analysis" technology should be promoted, using visual interfaces to show key drivers for a stock's inclusion in the portfolio (e.g., 70% of a semiconductor stock's inclusion is attributed to domestic substitution policies), improving investment decision transparency [8].

5.3 Ecosystem Construction and Global Competition

DeepSeek is building an "AI + finance" ecosystem with Wind and iFinD, focusing on three directions:

- **Multilingual intelligent research reports:** Real-time report generation in both Chinese and English has been realized, which supports the automatic extraction of key conclusions (such as the driving factors of gross profit margin changes) from 10-K financial reports and industry data. However, the accuracy of professional terminology in the Japanese and German markets still needs to be improved by 8%. It is planned to complete the special training of financial corpora in 10 languages by 2026.
- **Compliant data processing:** To meet cross-border data regulatory requirements (e.g., GDPR), a "data usable but not visible" module based on federated learning was developed, enabling model training without accessing raw data. Pilots will be launched in London and Singapore in Q4 2025 [10].
- **Edge deployment optimization:** Through FP8 quantization and model pruning, the core inference module's memory usage is compressed from 32 GB to 8.7 GB, supporting local operation on securities trading terminals with a response speed of <50 ms to meet high-frequency trading needs.

6 Conclusion

This study's multi-scale quantitative stock selection framework based on the DeepSeek large model achieves breakthroughs over traditional strategies through three core innovations: The adaptive Hurst threshold solves signal confusion during policy events; the high-frequency attention layer improves order book mutation signal capture efficiency; and the policy event factor enhances risk resistance in extreme markets.

Empirical results show that the strategy achieved a 29.3% annualized return with a 16.8% maximum drawdown from 2020 to 2024, significantly outperforming comparison benchmarks.

Future research will focus on three directions: Expanding feature dimensions through multi-modal fusion (integrating satellite images, ESG data); building a "human-machine collaborative decision system" allowing fund managers to adjust model parameters through natural language interaction; and participating in ISO/IEC AI financial standard formulation to promote technology output and global recognition [11]. The ultimate goal is to achieve a leap from "data-driven" to "cognition-driven" intelligent investment research, building a healthy human-machine symbiotic financial ecosystem.

References

1. Liao, H.L.: Performance optimization of DeepSeek MoE architecture in multi-scale prediction of stock returns. World J. Inf. Technol. **3**(2), 1–9 (2025). https://doi.org/10.61784/wjit3026
2. Zhang, W., et al.: TCN-based time series forecasting for quantitative investment. J. Financ. Data Sci. **7**(2), 112–134 (2025)
3. Shazeer, N., et al.: Outrageously large neural networks: the sparsely-gated mixture-of-experts layer. arXiv preprint arXiv:1701.06538 (2017)
4. DeepSeek-V3 Technical Report. DeepSeek-AI (2024). https://doi.org/10.48550/arXiv.2412.19437
5. Wang, J., et al.: Hierarchical routing in MoE models for financial time series. IEEE Trans. Knowl. Data Eng. (2025). https://doi.org/10.1109/TKDE.2025.3421891
6. Yu, F., Koltun, V.: Multi-scale context aggregation by dilated convolutions. arXiv preprint arXiv:1511.07122 (2015)
7. Liao, H.L.: A-share intelligent stock selection strategy based on the DeepSeek large model: technical routes, factor systems, and empirical research. Eur. J. Sci. Technol. **7**(2), 7–13 (2025). https://doi.org/10.61784/ejst3070
8. Li, H., et al.: Research on interpretability of financial large models based on MoE architecture. Financ. Technol. Res. **5**, 42–50 (2024)
9. Zhang, H., et al.: Social sentiment analysis for small-cap stocks. J. Behav. Financ. (2025). https://doi.org/10.1080/15427560.2025.2345678
10. GDPR Compliance in AI Models. European Data Protection Board (2024). https://edpb.europa.eu/
11. International Standards for AI in Finance. ISO/IEC JTC 1/SC 42 (2025). https://doi.org/10.1016/j.ijslm.2025.100012

Donation Management Transparency: Blockchain and RSA-Encrypted NFT Approach

L. K. Bang[1(✉)], P. H. T. Trung[1], N. Đ. P. Trong[1], and K. T. Ngan[2]

[1] FPT University, Can Tho city, Vietnam
bangle69.re@gmail.com
[2] FPT Polytechnic, Can Tho city, Vietnam

Abstract. This paper explores the application of blockchain technology to enhance transparency and accountability in donation management. Traditional donation systems often face challenges related to inadequate financial reporting, inefficient fund allocation, and a lack of oversight, which can lead to mistrust among donors. By leveraging blockchain's decentralized and immutable nature, along with smart contracts, RSA-encrypted NFTs, and IPFS, the proposed framework aims to address these challenges by ensuring secure, transparent, and automated transactions. The study evaluates several EVM-compatible platforms—BNB Chain, Fantom, Polygon, and Celo—assessing their capability to perform key operations such as transaction creation, NFT minting, and NFT transfer. Through a comparative analysis of transaction fees, the paper identifies the most cost-effective platforms for implementing blockchain-based donation management systems. The findings suggest that integrating these technologies can provide a robust solution for managing donations, fostering trust, and ensuring that funds are utilized as intended by donors.

Keywords: Blockchain · Donation · Financial Reporting · RSA-Encrypted NFT · IPFS · Smart Contracts · Decentralized Applications

1 Introduction

Charitable entities frequently encounter significant challenges in managing donations, with key issues surrounding transparency, accountability, and trust. Donors often lack visibility into how their contributions are gathered, distributed, and used, leading to diminished trust and concerns over the efficacy of their donations. Traditional approaches to donation management typically suffer from inadequate financial reporting, ineffective fund utilization, and lack of robust oversight, potentially leading to resource mismanagement or misuse [7,16]. Consequently, donors may feel detached from the results of their contributions, resulting in decreased trust and lower engagement in philanthropic activities.

S. Chen et al. (Eds.): METAVERSE 2025, LNCS 16159, pp. 75–86, 2026.
https://doi.org/10.1007/978-3-032-06323-6_6

Blockchain technology presents a viable solution by offering a decentralized and transparent system for donation management. Utilizing smart contracts, RSA-encrypted NFTs, and IPFS, blockchain-based methods can address these transparency challenges by facilitating secure, automated transactions that are indelibly recorded on the blockchain. This ensures that all donations are monitored from the point of donation to their final application, helping to uphold trust between donors and nonprofit organizations.

Blockchain technology has been proposed as a potential solution to these challenges due to its decentralized and transparent nature. By providing a public ledger that is immutable and verifiable, blockchain offers a way to document every step in the donation process, from the initial contribution to the final allocation of funds. This capability can help address many of the transparency and accountability issues that have plagued traditional donation management systems, as it allows donors and stakeholders to trace the flow of donations in real-time and ensures that all transactions are permanently recorded [14, 18].

Enhancing blockchain implementations with smart contracts facilitates the automatic distribution of funds, simplifying administrative processes and reducing the likelihood of fund mismanagement [6]. A significant security feature within this framework is the integration of RSA-encrypted Non-Fungible Tokens (NFTs), which bolster the system's security by safeguarding the identities of donors and recipients. This encryption ensures that while the donor's and recipient's information is securely protected, there is still a clear and verifiable trail of where funds are allocated, maintaining transparency throughout the transaction process [17]. Additionally, the adoption of the InterPlanetary File System (IPFS) complements blockchain by resolving data storage scalability challenges, efficiently managing the substantial data volumes generated by donation activities, and thus enhancing the overall reliability and efficiency of the system [4].

This paper contributes to the field of donation management by proposing a blockchain-based framework that integrates multiple technologies, including IPFS for decentralized storage, smart contracts for automated fund distribution, and RSA-encrypted NFTs for secure and verifiable transactions. By combining these technologies, the framework addresses scalability and data management challenges, ensuring that all donation-related data remains accessible, secure, and tamper-resistant. The study provides a comprehensive analysis of how this integrated approach can enhance transparency and accountability in managing donations, aiming to improve trust and ensure that funds are allocated according to donor intentions.

2   Related Work

2.1   Blockchain-Based Donation and Management Systems

These systems utilize the decentralized and immutable characteristics of blockchain to offer donors the ability to track their contributions in real time, ensuring that funds are used as promised. For example, Mhatre et al. describe a blockchain-based donation system that allows donations to be made directly to specific projects, with transactions recorded on a public ledger to enhance transparency [15]. Jadhav et al. explore the use of smart contracts in a blockchain-based donation system to automate the distribution of funds and reduce the risk of fraud, which in turn builds stronger trust between donors and beneficiaries [9]. Alex et al. discuss the benefits of blockchain in charitable activities, particularly its role in minimizing third-party intervention and ensuring that donations reach the correct recipients [2]. Ajmal et al. focus on how blockchain can empower donors by providing a platform that is both auditable and secure, which helps in ensuring that donations have a meaningful impact [1]. Furthermore, Hiremath introduces a decentralized application for charitable giving that operates on blockchain, creating a transparent and accountable system that offers direct interaction with recipients [8]. Collectively, these studies highlight the significant role blockchain technology can play in enhancing the transparency, efficiency, and reliability of charitable organizations.

2.2   Blockchain-Based Approach for Charity Management

Farooq et al. discuss a blockchain-based system that enhances the transparency and auditability of charity collections, addressing issues of mistrust in charitable donations through the use of crypto wallets and smart contracts for secure transactions [3]. Saleh et al. suggest a platform that uses blockchain technology to create a unified, transparent system for tracking donations, transactions, and donor details within charitable organizations [16]. Govindarajan et al. describe the development of a blockchain-based crowdfunding platform that aims to increase the transparency of fundraising activities, ensuring that funds are accessible only to verified entities, thus reducing fraud risks and boosting donor confidence [6]. Khallikunaisa et al. explore the use of a blockchain platform specifically designed for disaster relief and charity, employing smart contracts and cryptocurrencies to build a trustworthy, decentralized network that improves transparency and efficiency in charity management [12]. Furthermore, Funde et al. elaborate on combining blockchain with machine learning to create an advanced recommendation system for charities, which generates an accountability score to help donors identify reliable organizations, thereby enhancing transparency and building donor trust [4]. Together, these studies underscore the effectiveness of blockchain technologies in transforming the management and distribution of donations within charitable sectors, promoting a secure and transparent environment for both donors and beneficiaries.

2.3   Blockchain-Based Donation Tracking and Reporting Systems

Kotwal presents "CharityChain," a blockchain-based system that consolidates donation tracking, transaction management, and donor data into one platform, ensuring donors can transparently see how their contributions are utilized [14]. In a similar vein, Shaheen et al. introduce a blockchain-enabled system that allows donors to trace their contributions from the initial donation to final expenditure, thus rebuilding confidence in charitable organizations [18]. Khamkar et al.

further develop this idea with a blockchain-enabled charity application that provides transparent and accountable records of donations, enabling all stakeholders, including donors, charities, and recipients, to access real-time data on fund flows and utilization [13]. Sirisha et al. propose a blockchain solution designed for traceable donations, which utilizes smart contracts to streamline the donation process and enhance transparency for all parties involved [19]. Moreover, Herasymenko and Bachynska explore the use of blockchain in managing and distributing funds within charitable foundations to prevent fund misuse and increase trust among donors and beneficiaries [7]. Together, these research efforts emphasize the significant impact of blockchain technology in fostering a more transparent, secure, and efficient environment for managing and tracking charitable donations.

2.4   Advanced Applications of Blockchain in Charity Management

Saxena et al. explore a blockchain-based system for charity funding that converts real currency into virtual tokens, securing transactions and enhancing their traceability while employing algorithms to optimize and safeguard fund distribution [17]. Herasymenko and Bachynska investigate the application of blockchain for managing and distributing contributions within charitable foundations, using Ethereum smart contracts to ensure transparency and prevent fund misappropriation [7]. Funde et al. combine blockchain with machine learning to create a charity system that not only logs transactions but also assigns an accountability score to connect donors with credible organizations, thus improving transparency and security [4]. Gong and Sun introduce "ComputerBank," a community-oriented computer donation platform that merges blockchain, NFTs, and machine learning to manage donations transparently and securely, showcasing the adaptability of blockchain in varied settings [5]. Jain et al. design a blockchain-based financial management system for NGOs that utilizes decentralized technologies to deter corruption and enhance the traceability of transactions, thereby increasing donor confidence [10]. Khalil et al. offer a detailed examination of blockchain applications for charitable organizations, evaluating different blockchain platforms and their capability to heighten transparency and reduce fraud risks [11]. Collectively, these studies highlight the diverse and transformative potential of blockchain technology in improving the administration and allocation of charitable funds.

3   Approach

3.1   The Transparency Problem in Conventional Donation Management

In conventional donation management and fund distribution models, a lack of transparency frequently erodes trust between donors and recipients. Often, organizations do not provide sufficient or up-to-date details on how funds are collected and spent, causing donors to doubt whether their contributions are being used as intended or if the stated goals are being fulfilled. The infrequent or incomplete financial reporting adds another layer of uncertainty about the organization's financial practices and overall efficiency. This can result in funds being misallocated or used for purposes other than those initially specified, leading to inefficient use of resources. Inadequate financial oversight and auditing procedures further heighten the risk of fraudulent activities and mismanagement, as those in positions of authority may misuse funds for personal gain. Additionally, the traditional model tends to lack clarity on the impact of donations on recipients, which can leave donors feeling disconnected from the outcomes of their contributions. The use of intermediaries to handle and distribute funds introduces additional layers of complexity, which can increase operational expenses and reduce donors' direct oversight of their contributions. This reliance can create a feeling of separation and diminish trust, as donors often do not have the means to track or influence how their donations are used after they are given. Improving transparency in these processes is essential to building trust and ensuring that charitable efforts are both effective and meaningful. Blockchain technology offers a potential approach to these issues by providing a platform that is unchangeable and easy to verify, thus addressing many of the transparency problems and offering a more straightforward and accountable system for managing donations and distributing funds.

3.2   Phase 1: Blockchain-Based Approach for Donation Management

To enhance transparency and accountability in managing donations, a blockchain-based framework is proposed, as shown in Fig. 1. This framework incorporates several critical elements designed to ensure that each step in the donation process is transparent and can be verified.

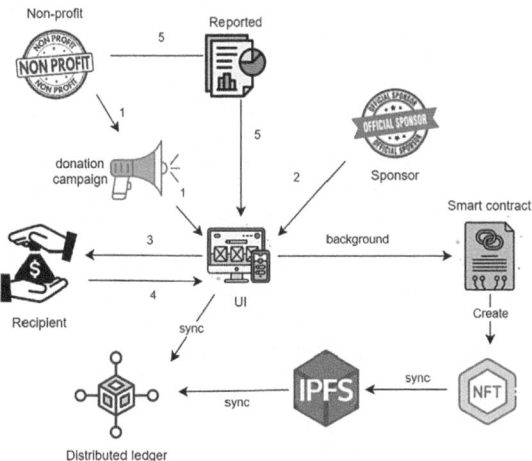

Fig. 1. Blockchain, IPFS, and NFT-enable architecture

The process of conducting a donation campaign using a blockchain-based system consists of several interconnected stages that promote transparency and accountability throughout. The process begins with the non-profit organization launching a donation campaign through a user interface (UI), where they provide key details such as the campaign's financial targets, how the funds will be used, and other relevant information. This information is then recorded on the blockchain, ensuring that all details about the campaign are both transparent and unchangeable.

Donors can browse different campaigns using the same UI and choose which ones to support. Donations are processed via smart contracts, which enable secure transactions and ensure that every donation is permanently recorded on the blockchain. After donations are collected, the funds are distributed to the designated recipients according to the campaign's plan. These transactions are also documented on the blockchain, allowing donors to verify that their donations are being utilized as intended. Once the funds have been received, recipients are encouraged to provide feedback and assessments regarding the support they obtained. This feedback is recorded on the blockchain, allowing donors and other stakeholders to access and review it. During the campaign, the non-profit organization is tasked with overseeing the management and reporting of the funds raised. This responsibility includes managing the distribution of funds and offering regular updates on financial reports and project developments. The process concludes with the non-profit organization reviewing the feedback and financial reports. This review process is intended to identify areas for improvement in future campaigns, promoting a mindset of continuous enhancement. The framework incorporates decentralized storage solutions, like the IPFS, to handle large datasets or files associated with the campaigns. Utilizing IPFS ensures that all data remains decentralized and accessible, which enhances the transparency and accountability of the donation process. Additionally, NFTs can be generated through smart contracts to create unique, verifiable records of each donation or to acknowledge donor contributions.

3.3   Phase 2: RSA-Encrypted NFT Access

The diagram Fig. 2 illustrates the use of RSA-encrypted NFTs within a blockchain-based system designed to manage and enhance transparency in donation activities. The process begins with a non-profit organization, which utilizes a smart contract to generate NFTs that are encrypted with RSA public keys to ensure the security and privacy of donation-related data. Public key A is associated with the non-profit, while public key B belongs to a sponsor or donor.

Initially, the non-profit organization creates an NFT, which represents a record of a donation or a tokenized asset. This NFT is encrypted using public key A, ensuring that only authorized parties within the non-profit can access the information. The encrypted NFT is then processed through the smart contract and made available on the blockchain. Subsequently, a detailed report on the donation, including its usage and impact, is generated and encrypted with public key B. This report is shared with the sponsor or donor, providing them

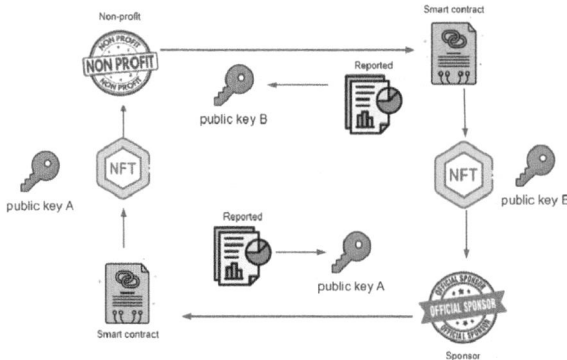

Fig. 2. RSA-encrypted NFT enable architecture

with a secure, verifiable record of how their contribution is being utilized. The sponsor, upon receiving the encrypted report and NFT, can verify the authenticity of the donation record using public key B. They can also generate their own encrypted report using public key A and send it back to the non-profit organization, allowing for a continuous exchange of verified information.

4   Implementation

The process for managing donations within a blockchain-based donation management system begins with the creation of a comprehensive data object (Fig. 3). This data structure contains crucial details about each donation, such as the amount donated, the donor's identity, the date of donation, and a unique identifier for each donation batch. It also includes in-depth descriptions of the intended use of the donated funds, the specific programs or projects they support, and any geographical or demographic information relevant to the donation's impact. This detailed dataset is essential for generating a corresponding Non-Fungible Token (NFT), which functions as a digital certificate to authenticate the donation and preserve a detailed record that remains accessible and verifiable throughout the entire management and reporting process.

The management of donations within a blockchain-based system starts with the formation of a detailed data object (Fig. 4). This data object captures essential information about each donation, including the donation amount, the identity of the donor, the date the donation was made, and a unique identifier for each batch of donations. It also provides detailed descriptions of how the donated funds will be used, the specific programs or projects they will support, and any relevant geographical or demographic details about the donation's intended impact. This comprehensive dataset is critical for creating a corresponding Non-Fungible Token (NFT), which serves as a digital proof of the donation. The NFT ensures the authenticity of the donation and maintains a complete and accessible record throughout the donation management and reporting process, enhancing transparency and accountability.

The entire donation management system utilizes technologies such as blockchain, IPFS, and RSA-encrypted NFTs. This combination not only secures all donation transactions but also ensures they are verifiable, thereby fostering greater trust and improving the effectiveness of the donation process. This approach provides a solid foundation for managing donations transparently, which is essential for maintaining accountability and operational effectiveness within charitable organizations.

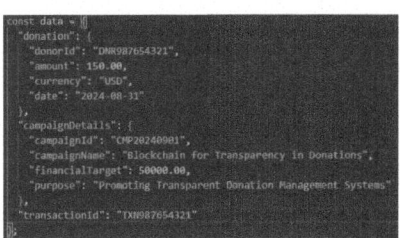

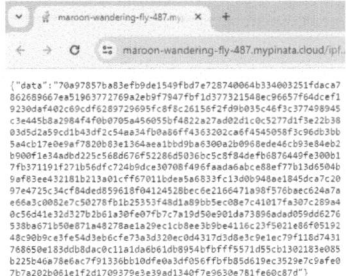

Fig. 3. JSON Data Structure of Transaction

Fig. 4. RSA Test Results

5　Evaluation

5.1　Evaluating RSA-Encrypted NFTs

The performance analysis examined the use of RSA-encrypted NFTs in a blockchain-based system designed to enhance transparency in donation management. This system employs blockchain technology, the IPFS, and RSA encryption to secure and handle data transactions, covering the entire process from the initial donation to the final allocation of funds. The evaluation focused on the encryption and decryption operations for two types of data: image files that serve to verify the authenticity of donations, and text records that detail transaction information and acknowledgments commonly found in donation activities.

The study consisted of ten trials to assess how RSA encryption was applied to these data types. Results showed that generating RSA keys for image files required an average of 2,461 milliseconds (ms), highlighting the substantial computational effort needed to establish a secure system environment. Image file encryption was faster, with an average time of 1,156 ms, which aligns with the system's need for efficient data processing. However, decrypting these image files took longer, averaging 3,442 ms, indicating the computational demands of the RSA decryption process and emphasizing the importance of balancing data security with operational efficiency (Table 1).

Table 1. Evaluation of Time for Image

RSA with image(ms)	1	2	3	4	5	6	7	8	9	10
Generating RSA key	2330	2206	2750	2314	2480	2218	2526	3790	2773	2378
Encrypting image	1436	848	913	890	1141	1422	1025	1036	1397	1355
Decrypting image	3234	3946	3337	3796	3379	3360	2449	3174	3830	3267

Similar observations were made for text data. Generating RSA keys for text took about 2,413 ms, showing a notable computational requirement at the start of the encryption process. Encrypting text data was slightly quicker, with an average time of 1,167 ms, maintaining consistency across different types of data. In contrast, decrypting text data took longer than decrypting images, with an average time of 3,561 ms. This difference may be due to the complex nature of text data, which can lead to extended decryption times (Table 2).

Table 2. Evaluation of Time Efficiency for Text

RSA with Text(ms)	1	2	3	4	5	6	7	8	9	10
Generating RSA key	2332	2257	2368	2259	2866	2736	2442	1947	2689	2151
Encrypting Text	1496	933	1363	1523	888	781	1483	825	1030	1520
Decrypting Text	3172	3810	3269	3218	4246	3483	4075	3228	3281	3329

These findings suggest that RSA encryption provides a consistent level of efficiency across different data types, which is important for preserving the integrity and security of a donation management system. However, the substantial computational resources required for key generation and decryption reveal the trade-offs involved in using RSA encryption for data security. The longer times needed for decryption, in particular, highlight the need to balance strong security measures with the requirement for timely access to data, which is critical for maintaining transparency and efficiency in donation management processes.

5.2   EVM-Supported Platforms Deployment

The administration of donation systems through blockchain technology necessitates a detailed assessment of transaction fees, as these costs significantly influence both operational expenses and the scalability of blockchain-based donation management solutions. This analysis conducts a comparative evaluation of transaction fees on four Ethereum Virtual Machine (EVM)-compatible platforms: BNB Chain, Fantom, Polygon, and Celo. The objective is to identify platforms that offer economical fee structures, potentially enhancing the operational efficiency and effectiveness of systems managing donations via blockchain.

The study explores how blockchain technology can improve the transparency and accountability of donation management systems, integrating features such as RSA-encrypted NFTs and the IPFS. The focus is on three primary operations: data generation, NFT minting, and NFT transfer. These functions are crucial for recording donation transactions, authenticating the validity of donation records, and ensuring the secure distribution of related digital assets across the network. The analysis further examines the feasibility and performance of the aforementioned four EVM-compatible blockchain platforms—BNB Chain, Fantom, Celo, and Polygon. Each platform is evaluated for its ability to facilitate the key operations necessary for efficient donation management systems. Particular emphasis is placed on the transaction processes' efficiency and cost-effectiveness, which are essential criteria in determining the most suitable platforms for constructing transparent and dependable systems dedicated to donation management.

5.3   Transaction Fee Analysis

Assessing transaction fees is essential when evaluating blockchain-based systems, especially within the realm of donation management. These fees play a significant role in determining the economic feasibility and operational viability of such platforms for all stakeholders. Transaction fees are necessary to reward validators or miners for their efforts in securing the network and facilitating transactions.

Our analysis concentrates on three fundamental operations crucial for the effectiveness of blockchain-based donation management platforms: generating transaction records, minting RSA-encrypted NFTs, and transferring RSA-encrypted NFTs. Each operation is vital to the entire donation management process on the blockchain, guaranteeing both secure and transparent record-keeping throughout the system.

Table 3. Transaction fee

	Transaction Creation	Create NFT	Transfer NFT
BNB	0.0273134 BNB ($14.51)	0.00109162 BNB ($0.58)	0.00057003 BNB ($0.30)
Fantom	0.00957754 FTM ($0.00)	0.000405167 FTM ($0.00)	0.0002380105 FTM ($0.00)
Polygon	0.006840710032835408 MATIC ($0.01)	0.000289405001852192 MATIC ($0.00)	0.000170007501088048 MATIC ($0.00)
Celo	0.007097844 CELO ($0.005)	0.0002840812 CELO ($0.000)	0.0001554878 CELO ($0.000)

Table 3 offers a comparative review of transaction fees for three critical operations on four Ethereum Virtual Machine (EVM)-compatible blockchain platforms: BNB Chain, Fantom, Polygon, and Celo, with token prices listed as of May 27, 2024. These operations, which include creating transactions, minting RSA-encrypted NFTs, and transferring RSA-encrypted NFTs, are fundamental for the management and safeguarding of donation records using blockchain technology.

BNB Chain incurs a higher transaction creation fee of 0.0273134 BNB, approximately $16.47, which could affect the affordability of frequent transaction activities. However, the fees for NFT creation and transfer are significantly lower, at 0.00109162 BNB ($0.66) and 0.00057003 BNB ($0.34) respectively. These reduced fees for NFT-related tasks indicate that BNB Chain may be a viable option for organizations handling large volumes of donation transactions represented as RSA-encrypted NFTs. Fantom offers one of the most competitive fee structures among blockchain platforms, with a transaction creation fee of only 0.00957754 FTM, which is relatively minimal. The fees for creating and transferring NFTs are lower still, at 0.000405167 FTM and 0.0002380105 FTM respectively, making them practically negligible. This cost structure is advantageous for scenarios that require high-frequency transactions, such as regular updates and exchanges of RSA-encrypted NFTs representing donations.

Polygon has a transaction creation fee of 0.006840710032835408 MATIC ($0.01), with extremely low fees for NFT creation and transfer at 0.000289405001852192 MATIC and 0.000170007501088048 MATIC respectively. These minimal fees facilitate the cost-effective scaling of operations, particularly for systems managing a wide variety of donation assets, thereby enhancing the affordability and use of RSA-encrypted NFTs in donation management. Celo, which prioritizes mobile accessibility and low-cost transactions, charges a transaction creation fee of 0.007097844 CELO ($0.005), with even lower fees for NFT creation and transfer at 0.0002840812 CELO and 0.0001554878 CELO, nearly negligible in cost. This fee structure is particularly beneficial for stakeholders in regions with limited financial resources, supporting effective donation management systems.

6   Conclusion

This study highlights the potential of blockchain technology to improve the management of donations by providing a transparent and secure platform that addresses the shortcomings of traditional systems. By incorporating smart contracts, RSA-encrypted NFTs, and IPFS, the proposed framework offers a comprehensive approach to ensuring transparency and accountability in the donation process. The analysis of EVM-compatible platforms, including BNB Chain, Fantom, Polygon, and Celo, demonstrates their varying capacities and cost efficiencies for handling critical operations involved in donation management. The findings suggest that careful selection of a blockchain platform based on its fee structure and operational capabilities can optimize the efficiency and effectiveness of donation management systems. The proposed framework not only enhances trust between donors and non-profit organizations but also ensures that donations are managed and allocated in a manner that aligns with donor intentions. Future work could further explore the implementation of such systems in real-world scenarios to validate these findings and refine the approach based on practical outcomes.

References

1. Ajmal, S., et al.: Empowering donors: how blockchain technology can help ensure their contributions reach the right recipients. In: 2023 International Conference on Business Analytics for Technology and Security (ICBATS). IEEE (2023)
2. Alex, S., Kanavalli, A., Ramdas, D.K.: Blockchain in philanthropic management. In: Advances in Data Mining and Database Management. IGI Global (2021)
3. Farooq, M., et al.: A framework to make charity collection transparent and auditable using blockchain technology. Comput. Electr. Eng. (2020)
4. Funde, K., et al.: Enhancing charity systems by leveraging blockchain technology and machine learning. In: 2023 11th International Conference on Emerging Trends in Engineering & Technology - Signal and Information Processing (2023)
5. Gong, E., Sun, Y.: Computerbank: a community-based computer donation platform using machine learning and nft. Signal Image Process. Trends (2022)
6. Govindarajan, S., et al.: Blockchain fundraising and charity platform. In: 2023 2nd International Conference on Vision Towards Emerging Trends in Communication and Networking Technologies (ViTECoN). IEEE (2023)
7. Herasymenko, O., Bachynska, V.: Blockchain technology for accounting and distribution of contributions from a charitable foundation. In: Technology Audit and Production Reserves (2021)
8. Hiremath, V.: Decentralised application on charity using blockchain. Int. J. Res. Appl. Sci. Eng. Technol. (2023)
9. Jadhav, V., Kadu, S., Kamble, C., Joshi, I., Gaikwad, S.: The implementation of donation system using blockchain. Int. J. Adv. Res. Sci. Commun. Technol. (2023)
10. Jain, M., Kaswan, S., Pandey, D.: A blockchain based fund management scheme for financial transactions in ngos. Recent Patents Eng. (2021)
11. Khalil, I., et al.: Blockchain and its implementation for charitable organizations. In: 2021 International Conference on Innovative Computing. IEEE (2021)
12. Khallikunaisa, et al.: Blockchain-based crowdfunding platform for disaster relief and effective charity. Int. J. Sci. Res. Sci. Technol. (2022)
13. Khamkar, A., et al.: Charitychain - a charity app built on blockchain. Int. J. Sci. Res. Sci. Eng. Technol. (2022)
14. Kotwal, P.: Charitychain a way for distributed charity donations. Int. J. Sci. Res. Eng. Manag. (2022)
15. Mhatre, P., et al.: Donation based system using blockchain. Int. J. Adv. Res. Sci. Commun. Technol. (2023)
16. Saleh, H., et al.: Platform for tracking donations of charitable foundations based on blockchain technology. In: 2019 Actual Problems of Systems and Software Engineering. IEEE (2019)
17. Saxena, A., et al.: Investigating the charity funding system using blockchain technology. In: 2022 IEEE World Conference on Applied Intelligence and Computing. IEEE (2022)
18. Shaheen, E., et al.: A track donation system using blockchain. In: 2021 International Conference on Electronic Engineering (ICEEM) (2021)
19. Sirisha, N., et al.: Proposed solution for trackable donations using blockchain. In: 2019 International Conference on Nascent Technologies in Engineering. IEEE (2019)

Decentralized Blockchain System for Ethical and Responsible AI in Generative Systems

Yathish Naraganahalli Veerabhadraiah[1,2(✉)]

[1] New York University, New York, NY 10012, USA
yn2426@nyu.edu

[2] Department of Computer Science and Engineering, Tandon School of Engineering,
New York University, New York, USA

https://yathish-naraganahalli-veerabhadraiah.streamlit.app/

Abstract. In the rapidly evolving landscape of artificial intelligence (AI), ethical governance frameworks are critical as AI systems become integral to sectors like finance and public governance. Generative AI systems, while transformative, pose significant ethical challenges, including bias, misinformation, lack of transparency, and misuse of intellectual property. Current centralized governance methods are opaque, unscalable, and raise questions about accountability and trust. This paper proposes a decentralized blockchain-based framework for ethical and responsible AI governance. Using blockchain features, such as immutable audit logs, data provenance tracking, bias auditing tools, content moderation platforms, and decentralized governance structures, the framework addresses key challenges in AI oversight. Smart contracts enforce ethical policies in real time, while token-driven incentives and staking mechanisms inspired by decentralized finance (DeFi) encourage honest participation. Decentralized Autonomous Organizations (DAOs) democratize AI governance, enabling multi-stakeholder decision-making. Key use cases include bias detection, content moderation, data provenance, audit logging, regulatory compliance, and decentralized governance. Challenges such as scalability, integration complexity, and the need for balanced human oversight are analyzed, with potential solutions like permissioned ledgers and cryptographic privacy techniques. This research charts a path toward morally aligned AI by combining blockchain's trust infrastructure with AI's transformative power, offering a blueprint for academia and industry to implement responsible AI monitoring. A decentralized and transparent approach can enhance trust in generative AI while respecting societal values.

Keywords: Generative AI · Blockchain · Decentralized Governance · Smart Contracts · Content Moderation · Bias Auditing · Permissioned ledger · DAO

1 Introduction

Rapid advancement and widespread adoption of generative artificial intelligence (AI) systems, such as large language models such as ChatGPT, have significantly

S. Chen et al. (Eds.): METAVERSE 2025, LNCS 16159, pp. 87–103, 2026.
https://doi.org/10.1007/978-3-032-06323-6_7

transformed a variety of industries. These technologies are now deeply integrated into sectors including finance, healthcare, and public governance, where they offer substantial decision-making capabilities and drive innovation. Despite these benefits, generative AI systems present a range of ethical and governance challenges. They are susceptible to producing biased outputs, spreading misinformation, generating fabricated content, and raising concerns about intellectual property rights and content ownership. The often opaque nature of these models further complicates efforts to ensure transparency, explainability, and accountability, making it difficult to trace the origins of specific outputs or assign responsibility when harm occurs.

Traditional approaches to AI ethics and oversight have relied on centralized mechanisms, such as human moderation, manual data filtering, and rules established by model developers. Although these methods can address some risks, they are frequently criticized for their lack of transparency, limited scalability, and concentration of decision-making power among a small group of stakeholders. This centralization raises important questions about who should define and enforce ethical boundaries for AI, and whether users and regulators can trust that AI systems are operating as intended. In response to these concerns, regulatory bodies around the world, including the European Union with its AI Act, are introducing new requirements for risk management, audit logging, and human oversight in AI systems.

Despite these regulatory developments, there remains a significant gap in the availability of governance frameworks that are both scalable and transparent and that can provide accountable oversight for generative AI. Existing solutions often fail to deliver verifiable compliance, multistakeholder participation, and tamper-proof records of AI behavior. To address these limitations, this article proposes a decentralized governance framework for ethical and responsible AI, using the characteristics of blockchain technology, immutability, transparency, and decentralization. The proposed architecture integrates smart contracts, decentralized autonomous organizations, and distributed ledgers to enable robust audit tracking, data provenance tracking, bias auditing, content moderation, and participatory governance.

By connecting established AI ethics principles such as fairness, accountability, and inclusivity with the technical capabilities of blockchain, this research aims to provide a foundation for trustworthy and compliant AI systems. The paper presents the architecture, discusses key use cases that include bias detection, content moderation, and regulatory compliance, and addresses challenges related to scalability, privacy, and integration. Through this approach, the work contributes to the ongoing discourse on responsible AI and offers a practical blueprint for implementing decentralized, transparent, and accountable AI governance.

2 Background and Theoretical Foundations

2.1 Responsible AI Principles for Generative Models

Fairness and Bias Mitigation: Generative models should steer clear of extending or magnifying social prejudices (gender, racial, etc.) found in training data. In artificial intelligence, bias can produce either unfair or damaging results. Best practices demand for dataset audits to find skew and bias detection in model outputs. Should biases be discovered, mitigating techniques such as data restructuring or model fine-tuning with bias penalties.

Transparency and Explainability: Stakeholders should to be able to grasp the reason behind an artificial intelligence generated output. While deep neural networks are sometimes opaque, responsible artificial intelligence promotes the least traceable logs or explanations for decisions. Audit trails are absolutely essential if one wants to examine AI behavior going backwards. In high-stakes fields, rules might call for recording of model decisions and data used for later analysis.

Accountability: When AI makes mistakes or causes harm, it should be obvious who is responsible. When using AI, organizations need to keep an eye on things and have the ability to step in and remove problematic models. Human-in-the-loop oversight is often recommended, in which human supervisors examine AI outputs in crucial situations such as when content has been identified as potentially sensitive.

Safety and Prevention of Harm: If generative AI is used inappropriately, it can generate harmful content, such as hate speech, explicit images, and dangerous instructions. To avoid damage, responsible AI entails putting in place moderation and content filtering systems. Additionally, there are issues with false information, such as deepfakes or AI-generated fake news, so systems should ideally have watermarking or verification features to identify AI-generated content.

Governance and Inclusivity: Rather than being created unilaterally by a single private company, the policies that regulate AI behavior (such as content guidelines and ethical constraints) should ideally be developed in an inclusive, multi-stakeholder manner reflecting societal values. This guarantees more widespread legitimacy and takes into account different viewpoints when defining what constitutes "ethical AI behavior."

Certain responsible AI measures are implemented by current state-of-the-art generative AI, such as ChatGPT, Claude, Grok. For instance, OpenAI employs a technique known as reinforcement learning from human feedback (RLHF) to align the model with human-provided guidelines and has moderation filters. But a lot of procedures are still secretive and proprietary. The demand for outside supervision and confirmation of these models' ethical compliance is rising. Here's where blockchain can be revolutionary: it can enable new governance structures that go beyond the AI developer alone and offer an external, tamper-proof, and shared system of record for data and decisions pertaining to AI ethics.

2.2   Blockchain Fundamentals and Decentralization Mechanisms

Immutability: It is very challenging to alter or remove data from a blockchain once it has been added and validated by the network. This produces tamper-proof logs that are perfect for an audit trail of AI activities, such as records of model outputs or changes. An AI provider cannot retroactively change logs to conceal wrongdoing without being discovered, thanks to immutability.

Transparency: Anyone can examine the data on public blockchains, such as Ethereum. Even private or permissioned blockchains that limit who can write to the ledger frequently grant authorized stakeholders read access. Due to this openness, third parties (such as regulators, auditors, or the general public) can examine and validate AI governance decisions or recorded events, which promotes trust. Additionally, it makes it possible for multiple parties to view the same record, preventing collective witnessing of AI behavior.

Decentralization and Consensus: A network of nodes uses consensus algorithms (like Proof of Work, Proof of Stake, or other Byzantine fault-tolerant techniques) to maintain the blockchain instead of a single authority. Decentralization means that no individual or organization can take control of or manipulate the records on its own. This could lead to distributed oversight in the context of AI, where a significant amount of independent observers (nodes) must concur on AI events or policy decisions that are recorded. This would lower the likelihood of cover-ups or biased enforcement by a central party.

Smart Contracts: These are self-executing programs stored on the blockchain that run when predetermined conditions are met. Smart contracts can be thought of as autonomous agents of governance wherre they can encode business logic or rules. For AI ethics, smart contracts could encode ethical policies or compliance checks that automatically trigger actions. Smart Contract Backpack allows developers to create production-ready and fully audited smart contracts, directly from the CLI in a matter of seconds which is ready to be deployed on the blockchain. ERC721 ERC721A ERC20 ERC1155 are some of the examples. Smart contracts allow blockchain technology to go beyond just managing cryptocurrencies by enabling the automation of complex agreements and transactions between parties without the need for intermediaries, essentially creating a platform for decentralized applications (dApps) across various industries, not just limited to digital currency exchange. Smart contracts can be considered an additional metadata field within a blockchain transaction, as they essentially provide extra information about the conditions and logic governing a transaction beyond just the basic transfer details, allowing for automated execution based on predefined parameters.

Incentives and Tokens (DeFi Mechanisms): Blockchain systems commonly use cryptographic tokens, which can represent assets, access rights, or governance votes. Smart contracts and tokens enable complex incentive schemes without centralized intermediaries, as demonstrated by Decentralized Finance (DeFi). These concepts are applicable to AI governance. For instance, a token could represent a stake or reputation for participants who audit AI outputs, much like DeFi protocols reward users for providing liquidity or security. Participants may receive tokens as a bond if they accurately identify problematic AI behavior; if they behave maliciously or carelessly, they may face penalties and forfeit their stake. Largescale AI monitoring can be crowdsourced through this type of incentive alignment. Additionally, a DAO's governance tokens can be used to vote on AI systems.

Identity and Roles: On a blockchain, entities are identified by their public keys, sometimes referred to as addresses. More sophisticated frameworks use decentralized identity (DID) standards or certificate systems to generate verifiable credentials on-chain. Maintaining an onchain registry of authorized stakeholders, such as auditors, developers, users, or verifiers, with specific permissions encoded via smart contracts, can help with AI oversight. For example, only certified auditors' keys may be allowed to decrypt and view certain sensitive logged data in order to preserve confidentiality when using the ledger. Additionally, this allows for the tracking of contributions: if a particular community member (identified by their address or DID) assists in identifying a bias issue, the system may record their assistance and potentially reward them with a token in an incentive registry.

DAO Governance Structures: A blockchain-based governance mechanism called a Decentralized Autonomous Organization (DAO) enables stakeholders who possess governance tokens to cast collective votes, often via smart contracts. DAOs have been used to oversee cryptocurrency projects, manage funds, and set rules for DeFi protocols. A DAO might serve as a governance council for AI monitoring, reviewing noteworthy occurrences, voting on revisions to AI ethics standards, or deciding whether to approve the deployment of models. Blockchain technology, which provides transparency and tamper resistance, is used to conduct votes and proposals. For crucial decisions, DAOs can also automatically enforce quorum and supermajority rules (e.g., requiring a broad consensus to approve a change in the AI's content policy).

3   Architecture Overview

This section presents a comprehensive overview of the proposed three-layer architecture for decentralized, ethical, and accountable governance of generative AI systems. The architecture is designed to integrate off-chain AI operations with on-chain blockchain governance and participatory decision-making through decentralized autonomous organizations (DAOs). Each layer is described below, along with its core components, intended functionality, and practical considerations (Fig. 1).

3.1   AI Orchestration Layer (Off-Chain)

The AI Orchestration Layer is responsible for managing the generative AI model (such as ChatGPT or similar foundation models) and the surrounding application logic. This layer operates off-chain and includes several key components:

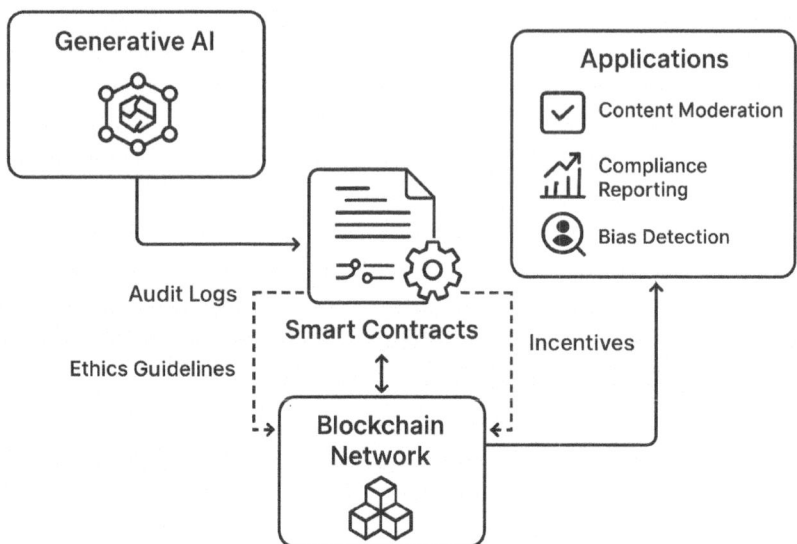

Decentralized Architecture for Responsible Generative AI Monitoring

Fig. 1. Three-layer architecture for decentralized AI governance using blockchain. The architecture includes the AI Orchestration Layer (off-chain), Blockchain Governance Layer (on-chain), and DAO Layer, which collectively enable ethical AI monitoring, policy enforcement, and decentralized decision-making

Context Handling and Input Processing: Inputs are pre-processed to ensure safety and compliance with ethical guidelines. This may involve context engineering, such as adding system instructions (guardrails) or screening prompts for malicious content before they are sent to the AI model.

Generative Model Inference: The core AI model generates responses based on the processed input. Post-Processing: The raw output from the AI model undergoes further processing, such as formatting and toxicity filtering. A critical feature here is the policy enforcement hook, which communicates with the blockchain governance layer to verify whether the output meets ethical and compliance requirements.

Response Delivery: If all checks are successful, the response is delivered to the user. If the output fails to meet compliance standards, appropriate actions are taken, such as issuing a refusal notice or providing a safe alternative completion.

Intended Functionality: This layer ensures that AI-generated outputs are screened for ethical and compliance violations before reaching the end user. It acts as the first line of defense in responsible AI deployment.

Limitations: While this design is robust in theory, the paper currently lacks empirical evidence or a prototype demonstrating its effectiveness in real-world scenarios. Future work should include simulation or pilot testing to validate these mechanisms.

3.2   Blockchain Governance Layer (On-Chain)

The Blockchain Governance Layer serves as the backbone for decentralized oversight and accountability. It is implemented on-chain and comprises several smart contracts and blockchain components:

Identity Registry Contract: This contract maintains a registry of all stakeholders (e.g., model owners, auditors, content moderators, end users, regulators) and their roles and permissions. Decentralized identity (DID) standards or off-chain verification may be used to ensure authenticity and prevent Sybil attacks.

Policy Contract: Ethical guidelines and compliance policies are encoded in this contract. It may include content guidelines (e.g., prohibiting hate speech or private data disclosure), thresholds for bias metrics, and cryptographic hashes of authorized model versions. While the contract serves as a compliance benchmark, it cannot perform complex AI calculations directly due to the computational limitations of smart contracts.

Audit Log Contract (Operation Registry): This contract immutably records significant AI activities, such as input reception, model responses, policy violations, and model updates. To maintain privacy, sensitive data can be stored off-chain, with only cryptographic hashes logged on-chain for integrity verification. This provides a tamper-proof audit trail for future review by auditors or regulators.

Incentive and Reputation Contract: This contract manages rewards and penalties to encourage honest participation in oversight tasks. For example, verifiers may receive governance tokens for accurately identifying problematic outputs, while malicious or consistently incorrect participants may lose reputation points or staked tokens. Staking mechanisms ensure that participants have "skin in the game," similar to validator incentives in decentralized finance (DeFi) systems.

Intended Functionality: This layer provides transparency, accountability, and compliance through immutable records, policy enforcement, and incentivized participation.

Limitations: Smart contracts are inherently limited in handling subjective or context-dependent ethical judgments, such as bias detection or nuanced content moderation. They rely on deterministic logic and often require off-chain oracles for complex evaluations, introducing potential vulnerabilities and trust issues. The scalability of logging high-frequency AI events on-chain remains a significant challenge, and proposed solutions such as batching, Layer-2 scaling, and selective logging require empirical validation.

3.3   DAO Layer

The DAO Layer enables participatory governance and collective oversight of the AI system. It consists of the following components:

Voting and Verification (Response Validation): For outputs flagged as sensitive or borderline, the system can initiate a decentralized verification process. The output (or its hash/ID) is forwarded to a network of human or AI verifiers, who vote on issues such as bias or compliance with ethical rules. The outcome is determined by a smart contract tallying the votes, and the output is either approved, blocked, or sent for revision.

DAO Governance Contract: This contract facilitates long-term governance by allowing stakeholders to propose and vote on changes to the AI system, such as model upgrades, incentive adjustments, or policy updates. Voting mechanisms may include token-weighted voting, one-entity-one-vote, quadratic voting, or multi-signature committees to balance power and prevent manipulation.

Intended Functionality: The DAO layer democratizes AI governance, ensuring that policies and ethical guidelines are developed and enforced collectively by a diverse set of stakeholders.

Limitations: DAO governance faces practical challenges, including low voter participation, potential for vote manipulation, and slow decision-making processes. Token-based voting can lead to centralization of power, while one-entity-one-vote systems are vulnerable to Sybil attacks. Achieving quorum and timely decisions is often difficult, especially in large or complex DAOs. Mitigation strategies such as quadratic voting, staking incentives, and multi-signature committees are proposed, but require further empirical testing.

Technical Mechanisms for Privacy, Policy-Enforcement, and Incentives On-Chain Privacy and Access Control: Smart contracts and the identity registry enforce role-based access to sensitive data and actions. Privacy-preserving techniques such as encryption, zero-knowledge proofs (ZKPs), and hybrid on-chain/off-chain storage are employed to balance transparency with data protection.

Automated Policy Enforcement: Smart contracts can serve as compliance monitors, issuing "permit" or "deny" tokens based on policy checks. However, their ability to enforce nuanced ethical rules is limited, and they often depend on off-chain components for complex evaluations.

Incentive Design (Staking and Rewards): Staking mechanisms and reputation systems incentivize honest participation in oversight and moderation tasks. Care must be taken to prevent centralization of power and ensure fair distribution of influence.

DAO Governance and Voting Schemes: Multiple voting mechanisms are available, each with trade-offs in terms of fairness, efficiency, and resistance to manipulation. The choice of mechanism should be tailored to the specific governance context and empirically evaluated.

Implementation Architecture of Blockchain-Based Responsible AI Monitoring

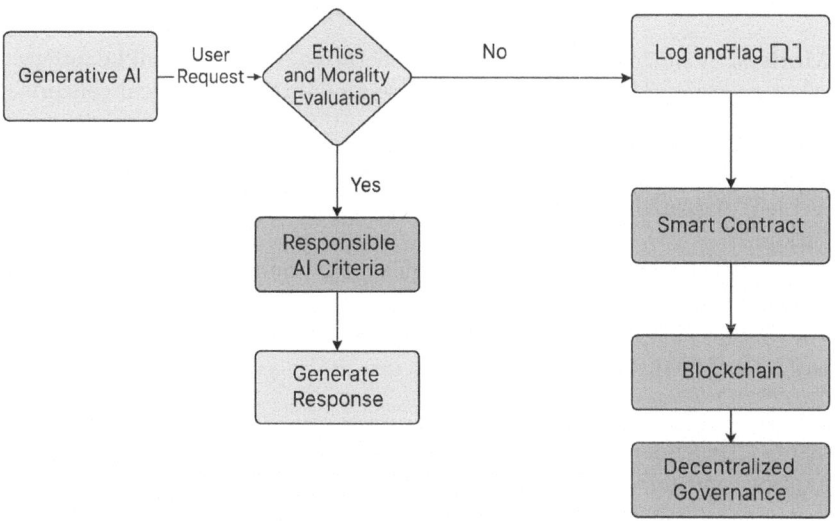

Fig. 2. Implementation flowchart of blockchain based Decentralized Governance

4   Methodology

This section outlines the experimental setup, evaluation methodology, and empirical testing procedures for the proposed decentralized blockchain-based governance framework for generative AI systems. The methodology is designed to rigorously assess the effectiveness, scalability, and practicality of the architecture across key use cases, and to provide a comparative analysis with traditional centralized governance systems (Fig. 2).

4.1   Experimental Setup

Blockchain Platform: The experimental framework will utilize both public and permissioned blockchain platforms to evaluate trade-offs between transparency, scalability, and privacy:

- **Ethereum (public, permissionless):** Chosen for its mature smart contract ecosystem, support for decentralized autonomous organizations (DAOs), and compatibility with Layer-2 scaling solutions. Ethereum testnets (e.g., Goerli, Sepolia) will be used for prototyping and simulation.
- **Hyperledger Fabric (permissioned):** Selected for scenarios requiring enhanced privacy, role-based access control, and higher throughput. Fabric's modular architecture allows for private channels and integration with enterprise systems.

- **Polygon (Layer-2 for Ethereum):** Used to assess improvements in transaction throughput and cost for high-frequency AI event logging.

AI Models: A range of state-of-the-art generative AI models will be integrated into the experimental setup to cover diverse modalities and ethical concerns:

- ChatGPT (OpenAI): For text generation, bias detection, and content moderation.
- DALL-E (OpenAI), Stable Diffusion: For image generation and provenance tracking.
- Claude (Anthropic), Bloom (BigScience): For multilingual and explainable AI scenarios.
- Other models (e.g., BERT for bias detection, Runway Gen-2 for video content) may be included for specific use cases.

Datasets: Benchmark datasets will be used to empirically test bias, content moderation, and provenance mechanisms:

- Bias Detection: COMPAS, Adult Income (UCI), Gender Shades, Civil Comments.
- Content Moderation: Jigsaw's Toxic Comment Classification, Hate Speech and Offensive Language, Reddit Corpus.
- Data Provenance: Open Images, COCO, and datasets with documented lineage and licensing.
- General Ethical AI: AI Fairness 360 (AIF360) datasets, ProPublica's Machine Bias, SQuAD, MS MARCO.

Tools and Frameworks

- Smart Contract Development: Truffle Suite, Hardhat, Remix IDE for Ethereum; Hyperledger Composer for Fabric.
- Blockchain Simulation and Benchmarking: Ganache (local Ethereum simulation), Hyperledger Caliper (performance benchmarking), SimBlock, BlockSim.
- AI Orchestration and Integration: Custom middleware to connect AI inference engines with blockchain event logging and policy enforcement.
- Privacy and Security: Libraries for zero-knowledge proofs (e.g., ZoKrates), encryption modules, and decentralized identity (DID) frameworks.

4.2   Evaluation Methodology

Simulation Scenarios: The system will be evaluated through a series of controlled simulation scenarios that reflect real-world applications of AI governance:

- High-frequency AI event logging: Simulate large volumes of AI outputs being logged on-chain to test scalability and latency.

- Policy enforcement: Test smart contract-based compliance checks for ethical rules (e.g., no hate speech, privacy protection).
- DAO-based decision-making: Simulate decentralized voting and verification for flagged outputs and policy changes.
- Privacy-preserving compliance: Evaluate the effectiveness of zero-knowledge proofs and hybrid on/off-chain storage for sensitive data.

Performance Metrics: The following metrics will be used to assess system performance and governance effectiveness:

- Scalability: Transaction throughput (TPS), latency, and system response time under load.
- Cost: Gas fees and operational costs for on-chain actions.
- Transparency and Auditability: Completeness and immutability of audit logs, ease of traceability for AI decisions.
- Privacy: Effectiveness of privacy-preserving mechanisms (e.g., ZKPs, encryption).
- Governance Participation: Voter turnout, proposal adoption rates, and decision finalization time in DAOs.
- Incentive Mechanism Effectiveness: Participation rates, accuracy of moderation/bias detection, and reputation system robustness.
- Compliance: Accuracy and completeness of compliance reports generated from blockchain logs.
- Comparative Metrics: Direct comparison with centralized systems on transparency, scalability, inclusivity, and trust.

Comparison with Centralized Systems

A baseline centralized governance system will be implemented for each use case, using traditional logging, moderation, and policy enforcement mechanisms. The decentralized blockchain-based system will be compared against this baseline using the metrics above, focusing on: Transparency and auditability of decisions and logs. Scalability and cost under high-frequency operations. Inclusivity and stakeholder participation in governance. Effectiveness in bias detection, content moderation, and compliance.

4.3   Empirical Testing of Use Cases

Each use case will be empirically tested as follows:

Bias Detection

- Setup: AI models will generate outputs using benchmark datasets (e.g., COMPAS, Civil Comments).
- Process: Inputs, outputs, and model parameters will be logged on-chain. Smart contracts will monitor for bias thresholds and trigger alerts or freezes.
- Evaluation: The accuracy of bias detection, the timeliness of alerts, and the effectiveness of DAO-based bias audits will be measured and compared to centralized audits.

Content Moderation

- Setup: AI-generated content will be evaluated using datasets like Jigsaw's Toxic Comment Classification.
- Process: Flagged outputs will be submitted to a decentralized moderation network, with decisions and rationales logged immutably.
- Evaluation: The fairness, accuracy, and transparency of moderation decisions, as well as the efficiency of incentive mechanisms, will be assessed against centralized moderation systems.

Data Provenance

- Setup: Training and inference data will be tracked using datasets with known provenance (e.g., Open Images, COCO).
- Process: Blockchain will record dataset origins, usage rights, and model versions. Tokenized data rights and NFTs will encode licensing rules.
- Evaluation: The completeness and accuracy of provenance records, and the system's ability to enforce licensing compliance, will be measured.

Audit Logging and Accountability

- Setup: All significant AI activities (inputs, outputs, policy checks, overrides) will be logged on-chain.
- Process: Audit logs will be reviewed for completeness, immutability, and privacy protection.
- Evaluation: The system's ability to provide tamper-proof, transparent, and privacy-preserving audit trails will be benchmarked against centralized logging.

DAO Governance

- Setup: Policy changes, moderation guidelines, and conflict resolutions will be proposed and voted on via DAO mechanisms.
- Process: Various voting schemes (token-weighted, quadratic, one-entity-one-vote) will be tested for fairness and resistance to manipulation.
- Evaluation: Governance participation rates, decision finalization times, and the inclusivity of stakeholder representation will be measured and compared to centralized governance models.

By systematically implementing and evaluating these scenarios, the methodology aims to provide a rigorous, data-driven assessment of the proposed decentralized governance framework's strengths, limitations, and real-world applicability for ethical and responsible AI systems.

5 Use Cases

Bias Detection: Bias is common in generative AI systems and often results in unfair outcomes. Blockchain can log all input data, parameters, and outputs immutably, enabling continuous bias monitoring through smart contracts and automated queries. Community-driven DAOs can crowdsource bias evaluations, with results transparently recorded on-chain. This approach increases accountability, incentivizes bias reduction, and provides a public, tamper-proof record of AI updates.

Content Moderation: Traditional, centralized moderation of AI-generated content is often opaque and subject to bias. By leveraging blockchain, moderation tasks can be decentralized and managed through smart contracts. Outputs flagged for review are assessed by a distributed network, and decisions are permanently recorded for transparency. Projects like GuardianScope demonstrate how economic incentives and community-based DAOs can ensure fair, tamper-evident, and democratic content moderation.

Data Provenance: Ethical AI requires transparency about the origins and usage rights of training data. Blockchain serves as a notary, recording dataset sources, usage permissions, and model versions with immutable timestamps. Tokenized data rights and NFTs can encode licensing rules, making it easier to manage intellectual property, conduct regulatory audits, and ensure compliant AI training and inference.

Audit Logging and Accountability: Blockchain provides an immutable audit trail of AI activities, including timestamps, user requests, model versions, and moderation actions. Smart contracts can trigger alerts or enforce rules based on logged events. This unalterable record supports real-time compliance monitoring, forensic audits, and independent verification by regulators, thereby building trust and ensuring legal responsibility.

Compliance: Meeting evolving AI regulations, such as the EU AI Act, requires robust record-keeping and evidence generation. Blockchain infrastructure enables secure logging of training data, bias audits, and outputs, accessible to regulators via smart contracts. Features like consent tracking and compliance dashboards support scalable, cross-border compliance and facilitate transparent regulatory reporting.

DAO Governance: Blockchain empowers participatory governance of AI systems through DAOs, where stakeholders—including developers, users, and ethicists—vote on policies, moderation guidelines, and conflict resolution. Smart contracts ensure transparent, multi-stakeholder participation, while mechanisms like quadratic voting and on-chain councils prevent power centralization. This distributed approach increases legitimacy and embeds ethical adaptability into AI governance.

6   Challenges and Limitations

The implementation of a decentralized blockchain-based governance framework for generative AI systems introduces a range of technical, operational, and ethical challenges. Addressing these limitations is essential to ensure the feasibility, effectiveness, and trustworthiness of the proposed architecture.

- **Blockchain Scalability** Scalability is a major technical challenge for blockchain networks, especially when used for high-frequency AI event logging. Generative AI systems like ChatGPT generate a vast number of queries and outputs per second, which public blockchains such as Ethereum cannot handle efficiently due to limited transaction throughput and high gas costs. This makes real-time, on-chain logging of every AI event impractical. Even permissioned or consortium blockchains, though offering higher throughput, may still become bottlenecked if each AI inference triggers a separate transaction. To address these issues, several mitigation strategies can be employed: batching and Layer-2 solutions (such as rollups or sidechains) aggregate multiple AI events into single transactions, significantly reducing on-chain volume and costs; event prioritization and selective logging ensure only critical events are recorded on-chain, with less important data stored off-chain; permissioned blockchains can provide higher throughput and lower latency, making them suitable for enterprise or regulated environments; and asynchronous operation allows AI processing and blockchain logging to be decoupled, enabling batch updates rather than immediate transactions. Despite these strategies, the feasibility of logging high-frequency AI interactions on-chain—particularly on public blockchains—remains uncertain and requires empirical validation through simulation or pilot deployments.
- **Reliance on Off-Chain Oracles:** The system depends on off-chain components (oracles) to feed results—such as whether an output is flagged as toxic—into the blockchain. This introduces potential vulnerabilities related to oracle security, data integrity, and trust.
- **Immutability and Flexibility:** Once deployed, smart contracts are difficult to modify, which can hinder the system's ability to adapt to evolving ethical standards or regulatory requirements.
  Mitigation Strategies:
- **Oracle Security:** Employing secure, decentralized oracle networks and cryptographic proofs (e.g., zero-knowledge proofs) can enhance the reliability and trustworthiness of off-chain data feeds.
- Automated Filters and Human-in-the-Loop Voting: Combining automated off-chain filters with human oversight (e.g., DAO-based voting) can improve the accuracy and fairness of AI output validation before logging on-chain.
- **Incremental Adoption:** Gradually expanding the scope of smart contract-based governance, starting with simpler use cases, allows for iterative improvement and risk mitigation.
- **Privacy and Transparency Trade-Offs**
- Balancing transparency and auditability with the protection of sensitive data is a core challenge in blockchain-based AI governance:

- Sensitive Data Exposure: Logging user inputs, AI outputs, or training data on a public blockchain can compromise privacy and violate data protection regulations.
- **Transparency vs. Confidentiality:** While blockchain promotes transparency, it may conflict with the need to keep proprietary or personal information confidential.
  Mitigation Strategies:
- Zero-Knowledge Proofs (ZKPs): ZKPs enable the system to prove compliance with ethical policies without revealing the underlying data, thus preserving privacy while maintaining verifiability.
- Encryption and Access Control: Sensitive data can be encrypted on-chain, with decryption keys accessible only to authorized stakeholders (e.g., auditors or regulators).
- Hybrid On-Chain/Off-Chain Designs: Storing only cryptographic hashes or compliance proofs on-chain, while keeping actual data off-chain, ensures data integrity without exposing sensitive information.
- **Adversarial Risks and Manipulation**
  Decentralized governance systems are susceptible to adversarial attacks and manipulation:
- Collusion and Sybil Attacks: Malicious actors may collude or create fake identities to manipulate DAO votes or governance decisions.
- Token Centralization: Token-based voting can lead to power concentration among a few stakeholders, undermining the inclusivity and fairness of the system.
  Mitigation Strategies:
- Staking and Incentive Mechanisms: Requiring participants to stake tokens as collateral, with penalties for dishonest behavior, can deter manipulation.
- Reputation Systems: Tracking the reputation of verifiers and auditors incentivizes honest participation and penalizes malicious actions.
- Randomized Committees: Using randomly selected committees for decision-making reduces the risk of collusion.

7   Future Work

Future work includes zk-proof-based privacy-preserving audits, cross-platform DAOs, incentive-based trust scoring, and provable AI safety on-chain.

- **AI-Blockchain Integration:** Research into running lightweight AI models or generating verifiable AI output proofs (e.g., zk-SNARKs) on-chain can offer provable transparency and logic enforcement.
- **AI-Assisted Governance:** With human supervision to prevent feedback loops, AI can help DAOs by examining logs, bringing governance concerns to light, and modeling the effects of proposed policies.
- **Cross-Platform Governance:** Federated blockchain systems had the potential to standardize AI oversight across jurisdictions and providers, fostering transparency and industry-wide standards.

- **Incentive-Driven Governance (DeAI):** Decentralized bounties, prediction markets, and rewards for moral AI conduct and vulnerability disclosures can be modeled using economic models from DeFi.
- **Legal and Social Harmonization:** User trust and regulatory alignment can be improved by incorporating legal contracts into smart contracts and researching public opinion.
- **Privacy-Preserving Accountability:** Using technologies such as zero-knowledge proofs and homomorphic encryption could protect privacy while upholding accountability.
- **AI Alignment through Collective Oversight:** DAOs can assist in guiding moral frameworks and AI training objectives, transforming societal values into machine-aligned objectives.
- **Multimodal AI Governance:** In order to handle deepfakes, intellectual property, and physical actions, governance models need to adjust to AI in visual, aural, and robotic modalities.
- **Benchmarking Impact:** To assess the ways in which decentralized oversight enhances public trust, moderation accuracy, and bias reduction, empirical research is required.

8   Conclusion

The convergence of artificial intelligence and blockchain technology is reshaping the landscape of ethical AI governance. By decentralizing the monitoring and oversight of generative AI systems, greater legitimacy and inclusivity can be achieved in defining ethical standards, as input from diverse cultures, disciplines, and stakeholders is enabled. This paper has demonstrated that integrating decentralized blockchain mechanisms such as smart contracts, immutable ledgers, and DAO-based governance—can provide open, accountable, and community-driven frameworks for responsible AI. The proposed architecture supports key functions including regulatory compliance, data provenance, content moderation, and bias auditing, all while enhancing transparency and trust. Although challenges remain, particularly regarding scalability, privacy, and integration complexity, the combination of blockchain and AI offers a promising pathway toward systems that are not only technically advanced but also aligned with human values and societal expectations. Blockchain is positioned not merely as a transactional tool, but as a governance technology uniquely suited to address emerging issues in AI ethics. As the field evolves, decentralized, blockchain based responsible AI monitoring is expected to play a pivotal role in fostering AI systems that are equitable, trustworthy, and operated in the public interest, thereby paving the way for the next generation of ethical and transparent artificial intelligence.

References

1. Li, X., Wang, X., Kong, T., et al.: From bitcoin to solana–innovating blockchain towards enterprise applications. In: International Conference on Blockchain, pp. 74–100. Springer, Cham (2021). https://doi.org/10.1007/978-3-030-96527-3_6

2. Liu, Y., Lu, Q., Zhu, L., Paik, H.: Decentralised governance for foundation model based AI systems: exploring the role of blockchain in responsible AI. IEEE Softw. (2024)
3. McKay, C.: Casper and IBM Partner to Apply Blockchain for AI Governance. Maginative (2024)
4. KPMG Insights: Blockchain and Generative AI: A Perfect Pairing? (2023)
5. Liu, Y., Lu, Q., Zhu, L., Paik, H.: Decentralised governance-driven architecture for foundation model based AI systems. arXiv:2308.05962 (2024)
6. Friedl, P., Morgan, J.: Decentralised content moderation. Internet Policy Rev. **13**(2) (2024)
7. Sumit, K.: 5 Groundbreaking AI projects using blockchain. DEV (2025)
8. Willson, M.: Blockchain Can Monitor Bias in AI Models. Blockchain Council (2024)
9. OpenLedger: Decentralized Infrastructure for AI and Data Provenance (2024)
10. Ocean Protocol: Privacy-Preserving Data Sharing for AI (2024)
11. Kaal, W.A.: Decentralized AI Governance: A Web3 Perspective. Minnesota Legal Studies Research Paper No. 22-11 (2023)
12. European Commission: EU Artificial Intelligence Act (2023)
13. Allen, M.C., Bernstein, S.J.: AI governance via Web3: how blockchain can ensure responsible generative AI. Stanford J. Blockchain Law Policy **2** (2024)
14. Partnership on AI: Tenets for Responsible AI (2022)
15. IEEE: Ethically Aligned Design: A Vision for Prioritizing Human Well-being with Autonomous and Intelligent Systems (2019)
16. UNESCO: Recommendation on the Ethics of Artificial Intelligence (2021)
17. Coeckelbergh, M.: AI Ethics: The Basics. Routledge, London (2020)
18. European Commission: Ethics Guidelines for Trustworthy AI (2019)
19. Allen, M.C., Bernstein, S.J.: AI governance via Web3: how blockchain can ensure responsible generative AI. Stanford J. Blockchain Law Policy **2** (2023)
20. Buolamwini, J., Gebru, T.: Gender shades: intersectional accuracy disparities in commercial gender classification. Proc. Mach. Learn. Res. **81**, 1–15 (2018)
21. ProPublica: Machine Bias: There's Software Used Across the Country to Predict Future Criminals. And it's Biased Against Blacks (2016)
22. AI Fairness 360: Open Source Toolkit for Detecting and Mitigating Bias in Machine Learning Models (2023)
23. Open Images Dataset: Google AI (2023)
24. Lin, T.-Y., et al.: Microsoft COCO: common objects in context. In: Fleet, D., Pajdla, T., Schiele, B., Tuytelaars, T. (eds.) ECCV 2014. LNCS, vol. 8693, pp. 740–755. Springer, Cham (2014). https://doi.org/10.1007/978-3-319-10602-1_48
25. SQuAD: Stanford Question Answering Dataset (2023)
26. MS MARCO: Microsoft MAchine Reading COmprehension Dataset (2023)
27. Blockchain Council: Blockchain for AI Governance: Use Cases and Challenges (2024)
28. Hyperledger Caliper: Performance Benchmarking for Blockchain Networks (2024)
29. ZoKrates: Zero-Knowledge Proofs for Ethereum (2024)
30. Partnership on AI: Responsible Practices for Synthetic Media (2023)
31. Coeckelbergh, M.: AI Ethics. MIT Press, Cambridge (2020)
32. European Commission: Proposal for a Regulation Laying Down Harmonised Rules on Artificial Intelligence (Artificial Intelligence Act) (2021)

The Interplay Between Cryptography and Blockchains: A Case Study of Ethereum

Zhexiu Tu$^{(\boxtimes)}$ (iD) and Charles Pizzuti (iD)

Sewanee: The University of the South, Sewanee, TN 37383, USA
{zhtu,pizzucd0}@sewanee.edu

Abstract. Digital trust management in modern times uses blockchain technology and cryptography for building trust through dependable security protocols which operate decentralization. Basic blockchain operations receive core security through cryptographic authentication methods which validate data parts and verify users before enabling mutual agreement mechanisms for unalterable data storage. An evaluation of blockchain operation cryptography needs to analyze the Ethereum network. Ethereum achieves decentralized transparent operations through cryptographic resources that consist of hash functions and elliptic curve cryptography and digital signatures as well as zero-knowledge proofs which operate as emerging protocols.

Ethereum supports transaction approvals and identity safeguards because its cryptographic structure makes trustless operation of smart contracts automatic. Ethereum intends to develop Ethereum 2.0 features with zk-SNARKs along with BLS signatures as its vital technical bases for scalability and privacy system enhancements. Research on new cryptographic techniques will explore cryptographic process protection methods for Ethereum 2.0 since its cryptographic vulnerabilities remain unaddressed. The evaluation demonstrates that secure decentralized digital platforms generate equivalent worth from cryptographic and blockchain technologies.

Keywords: Ethereum · security · blockchain · cryptography

1 Introduction

Blockchain technology serves as a revolutionary digital innovation which changes multiple sectors such as financial operations and supply chain functionality as well as healthcare management and governance systems. Blockchain started its life as a system for decentralized currencies but developers later created it as foundational infrastructure for different decentralized applications. The blockchain technology creates secure storage solutions because it distributes and defends data from tampering thus enabling trustless systems to work without centralized management.

The reliability and trustworthiness of blockchain technology heavily depend on cryptographic operations as the fundamental component. Cryptographic approaches form an

S. Chen et al. (Eds.): METAVERSE 2025, LNCS 16159, pp. 104–114, 2026.
https://doi.org/10.1007/978-3-032-06323-6_8

undetectable infrastructure enabling blockchains to execute their functions. The application of cryptographic techniques protects decentralized systems by making such systems both feasible and secure and operationally efficient.

Ethereum leads the many blockchain platforms with its programmable smart contracts because these smart contracts increase blockchain usage possibilities significantly. Ethereum uses different cryptographic protocols that provide security features to both smart contracts and decentralized applications (dApps). This document explores how cryptographic solutions work together with Ethereum's blockchain technology through investigation of their enabling role for core system features while studying deficits in decentralized environments going forward (Fig. 1).

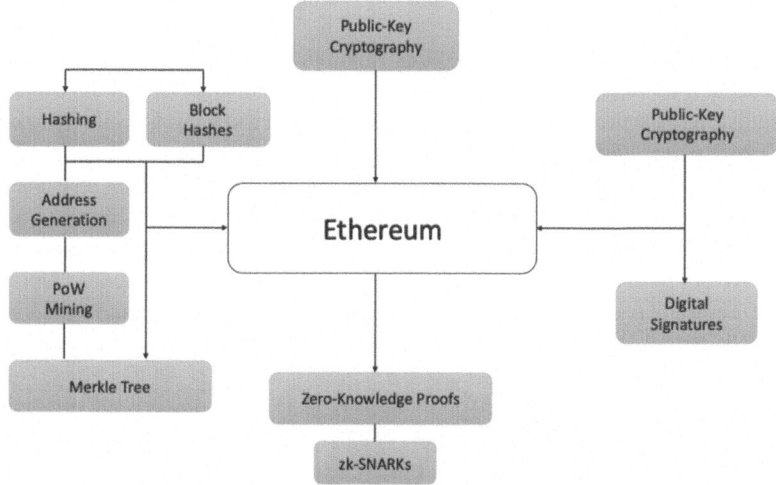

Fig. 1. Overview of Ethereum's Cryptographic Framework

2 Overview of Blockchain Technology

The researcher [1] says distributed ledger technology (DLT) blockchain lets users establish secure, transparent and unalterable data records across decentralized computer systems known as nodes. A block within the blockchain contains multiple transactions together with a timestamp while featuring an encoded cryptographic hash from the previous block to create a secure time-stamped chain that cannot be modified. The algorithm ensures data records stay permanently protected because changes made to any block require consensus agreement spanning most network computers and alteration of subsequent blocks.

Blockchain operates as several peer-to-peer independent nodes which diverges from database structures through trust-building approaches based on Proof of Work (PoW) and Proof of Stake (PoS). Blockchain remains the best technology option to achieve decentralization of trust since it enables cryptographic tools for secure voting systems and digital identity systems and other similar applications.

3   Cryptographic Fundamentals in Blockchain

Blockchain systems function on the cryptographic security model deployed across their infrastructure. Ethereum implements three main cryptographic elements within its system:

3.1   Hash Functions

The blockchain technology such as Ethereum requires hash functions as essential cryptographic components to perform its operations. The mathematical computation called hash generates an output from any input length to a definite string of hexadecimal characters. Keccak-256 which belongs to the SHA-3 family functions as the principal hashing algorithm for Ethereum networks [2].

A cryptographic hash function requires four fundamental traits made up of determinism backed by pre-image resistance followed by second pre-image resistance and lastly collision resistance. The property of pre-image resistance makes it impossible to perform practical calculations that restore original input data from hash output values. The combination of second pre-image resistance together with collision resistance prevents distinct input options from producing matching output values in the system. Hash functions in Ethereum perform multiple crucial operations throughout the system.

Next blocks receive their hash value from the header of their preceding block. The secure chronological sequence gets formed through hash function calculations. Tampering would be detected immediately because any harm to one block would render invalid the hashes of all succeeding blocks.

Early Ethereum operations based on Proof of Work (PoW) allowed miners to compete for solving computational hashing puzzles. The network system gained protection from spam and malicious actors through this security feature.

Ethereum generates unique addresses for users by computing public key hashes thus maintaining user privacy.

Merkle trees combine all transactions from a block through hash functions as data structures to enable both secure and efficient assessment of substantial dataset contents.

Persistent data security is preserved in Ethereum through hash functions which perform these crucial tasks. The cryptographic framework of Ethereum depends on hash functions to remain indispensable as it proceeds with newer consensus models and privacy features implementation (Fig. 2).

3.2   Public-Key Cryptography

The security foundation of Ethereum depends on public-key cryptography because it functions as asymmetric cryptography. The two fundamental cryptographic keys of public-key cryptography serve as opposites because users employ their matching private or public key to encrypt or decrypt respectively. Every participant receives access to the public key yet only its owner holds exclusive knowledge about the private key [3].

The authentication features of Ethereum operate with public-key cryptography which verifies transactions using this security system. Users create Ethereum accounts through the implementation of Elliptic Curve Digital Signature Algorithm (ECDSA) on

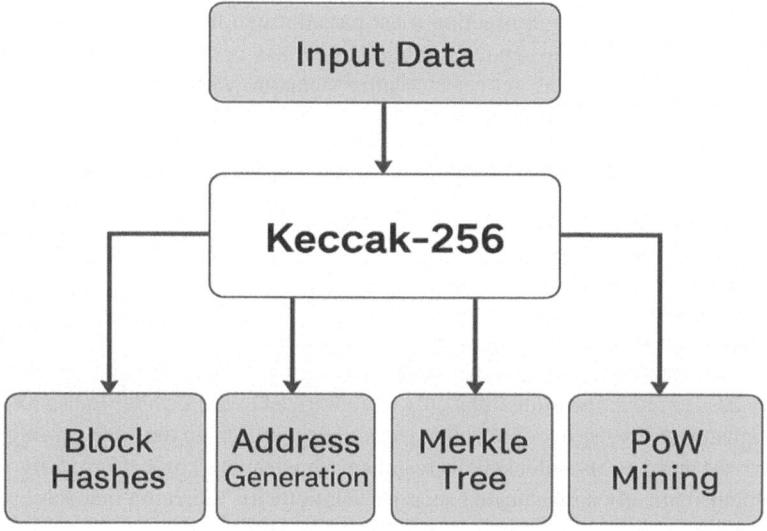

Fig. 2. Role of Hash Functions in Ethereum

secp256k1 curve which generates their private-public key pairs. The Transaction authentication process depends on the private key because the signature function can only be executed by the key holder to prove network identity. The production of Ethereum addresses happens when the Keccak-256 hashing function operates on public keys resulting in a hexadecimal string network identifier.

The network requires all submitted transactions to have their digital signatures verified through the public keys of transaction senders. A properly signed transaction enables the network to verify transaction validity because it ensures both data authenticity and sender identity based on their possession without revealing their private key details.

The implemented model protects against false operation claims as it secures user safety through operations authentication while eliminating trust-dependence in the system. Ethereum relies on public-key cryptography since its decentralized nature requires trust mechanisms between users while sustaining trustless peer-to-peer transactions without central administrator supervision. The security platform of Ethereum functions based on these fundamental reasons.

3.3 Digital Signatures

Digital signatures operate as the main cryptographic feature within Ethereum Blockchain technology implementation. The digital signature system enables authorized users to validate digital content through a secure mechanism which keeps their personal keys untouched. Within Ethereum digital signatures depend on the Elliptic Curve Digital Signature Algorithm (ECDSA) that uses the secp256k1 curve which bitcoin along with other blockchain platforms standardize.

A user signs digital messages with their private key whenever they send data to the Ethereum network. A network transaction broadcast includes a signature that uses the private key to create. Every transaction must pass through the validators who authenticate the signature using the sender's public key to also confirm its original form has remained intact. Transactions get rejected after signature verification reveals any verification failure. Verification of signatures serves as a shield against reputative claims because the sender keeps no power to disclaim sending the transaction.

Signature composition requires r and s components that result from mixing the private key of the sender with transaction information through processing the data. On Ethereum signatures hold an additional parameter called v that helps public key extraction while minimizing data duplication requirements for address verification.

Digital signatures serve three essential functions by providing protection of transaction data integrity in agreement with identity verification process and user permission management. Smart contract execution depends on digital signatures because they restrict access to predefined functions only to authorized users. Besides transaction execution signatures serve as a tool to authorize actions in off-chain message signing while removing the need to use blockchain resources thus saving costs. Digital signatures deliver mathematically sophisticated security solutions for Ethereum that achieve trust across a trustless system thereby implementing blockchain's decentralized principles (Fig. 3).

3.4 Merkle Trees

Blockchain systems implement Merkle trees as cryptographic structures through which users achieve secure data verification efficiently. Ralph Merkle introduced this data structure in 1979 hence people call it Merkle trees which transforms data blocks into cryptographic hashes to store within leaf nodes that spread up through non-leaf nodes

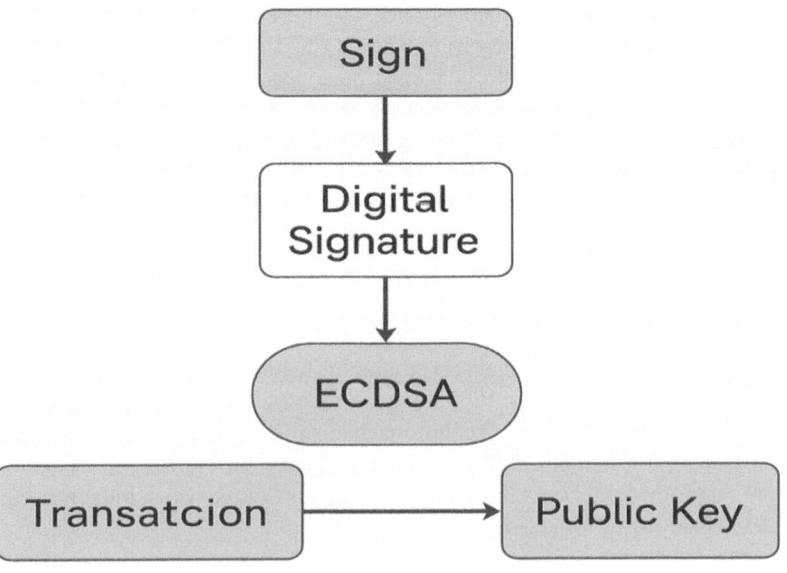

Fig. 3. Digital Signature Process in Ethereum

from leaf to root. The hash processing sequence produces a single root hash identified as the Merkle root that precisely signifies the transaction status in every block.

Ethereum makes use of Merkle trees to handle and validate extensive data collections through efficient operations for verifying block transaction records along with ledger balances and smart contract information. Ethereum implements Merkle Patricia Trie as its data management solution that unites Merkle tree efficiency with trie structure ordering abilities. The system helps create efficient verification systems that operate quickly when combined with quick validation capabilities that support Ethereum operations (Fig. 4).

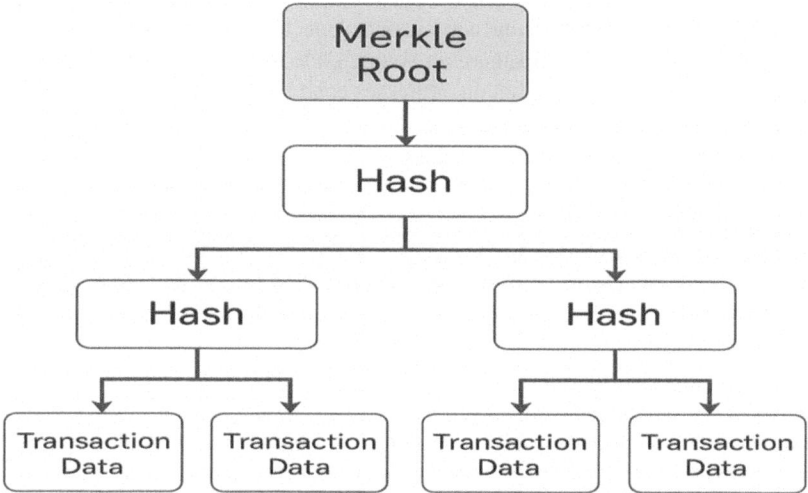

Fig. 4. Merkle Tree Structure in Ethereum

The main benefits which Merkle trees provide include:

1. Users need only request small Merkle proofs for efficient block verification instead of downloading full blocks because Merkle proofs provide paths of hashes connecting leaves to root hashes [4].
2. The modification of any single transaction produces hash modifications that force alterations throughout all the parent hashes up to the root. The amplifying modification process enables users to detect every minor change in the system.
3. The data transfer needs at Ethereum are reduced through Merkle trees which allows nodes to synchronize efficiently while enabling the network to scale for light client capabilities.

Data integrity enhancement along with proof efficiency and trustless verification functions in Ethereum's decentralized ecosystem rely on Merkle trees as its essential cryptographic structure.

4   Cryptography in Ethereum: Case Study

4.1   Smart Contracts and Solidity

The smart contracts on Ethereum platform serve as a groundbreaking development which enables decentralized applications (dApps) to perform automatically while removing dependency on central entities. The Ethereum blockchain maintains self-executing contract code which operates by spreading identities to all nodes on its network. Solidity serves as Ethereum's main programming language for developing smart contracts since it derives its features from JavaScript and combines elements of Python and C++ [5].

Through Solidity developers can establish their own contract definitions which cover functions together with variables and access control mechanisms. After code compilation generates EVM bytecode from Ethereum source code to establish deployment on the Ethereum blockchain. The blockchain addresses each smart contract uniquely thereby enabling it to operate autonomously while keeping track of digital assets that include Ether and tokens securely without needing trust.

Cryptography stands essential for safeguarding the both deployment and operational process of smart contracts. All digital transactions related to smart contracts need user validation through private key signatures to ensure authenticity and prevent later denial. The implementation of hash functions occurs within smart contracts to perform authentication of user credentials and validate input data and create unique system identifiers.

Solidity offers two distinct security features through event logging for emission of contract records and modifiers enforcing extra security measures including time-limited functionality and access rules. Through a combination of the Ethereum consensus mechanism with these features the system achieves transparent execution of uniform code through tamper-proof mechanisms across all nodes.

The immutability of deployed smart contracts necessitates strict testing protocols because any crypto-related flaw including reentrancy attacks and integer overflows would enable an attack.

By merging cryptography with smart contracts within Ethereum users can achieve tamperproof automated digital agreements which transform financial operations and supply chain and insurance and real estate industries (Fig. 5).

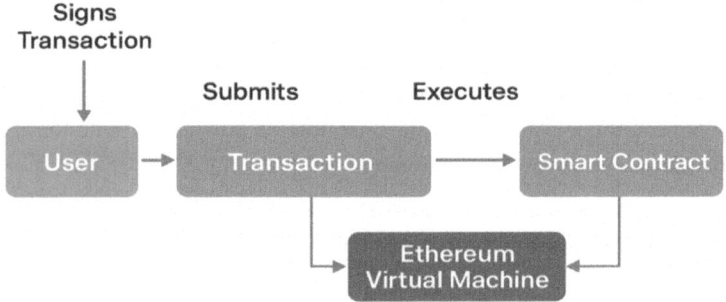

Fig. 5. Smart Contract Deployment and Execution Workflow

4.2 Account and Address Security

The account and address security mechanisms of Ethereum are essential to protect users' financial assets through privacy measures. A cryptographic hash function converts each Ethereum public key into a separate account address which makes them unique. Users can identify themselves through addresses that allow sending or receiving of ETH together with smart contract interactions on the blockchain. Applying Elliptic Curve Digital Signature Algorithm (ECDSA) on secp256k1 cipher users generate their essential key pair including both public and private keys.

A user needs their private key to receive authentication when performing blockchain transactions since it functions as the authorizing security credential. Keeping the private key safe and secret is important because it gives total control to whoever possesses it for the financial assets linked to a specific public address. The loss or theft of a private key results in permanent asset disappearance since there exists no authority capable of recovering the funds. The decentralized management of Ethereum signals both benefits and weak points to the system.

The computation of Ethereum addresses starts with Keccak-256 cryptographic hashing of public key data. The hash function protects public addresses from possible attacks because hackers cannot easily derive private keys from them. This strengthens security measures. Each Ethereum address consists of 160 bits represented through a hexadecimal system that provides cryptographic protection despite its measurement flexibility.

Ethereum enhances its account security through digital signatures which enable verification of transactions. Users need to authenticate transactions with their private keys as a necessary step to transmit them throughout the network. Every transaction participant can check the authenticity of transactions through public keys to ensure that only authorized address owners can make transfers.

Users protect their Ethereum accounts through storing private keys securely within hardware wallets while encrypting them using software wallets to prevent losses from phishing and hacking troubles.

4.3 Zero-Knowledge Proofs (Zk-SNARKs)

Users can validate the validity of statements through Zero-Knowledge Proofs (ZKPs) without providing the recipient details beyond those demonstrated by the proof itself. Blockchain technology chooses zk-SNARKs or Zero-Knowledge Succinct Non-Interactive Arguments of Knowledge because they serve as vital cryptographic proof methods to balance private data protection and system transparency [6].

The zk-SNARK protocol provides improved evidence verification through statements that disclose no prejudicial related facts. zk-SNARKs enable Ethereum to execute secret smart contracts and privacy-protecting transactions by letting users prove particular information while keeping the actual details hidden. The technology serves important functions when operators need to hide essential transaction data that includes sender information combined with payment amount and receiver identification.

One key strength of zk-SNARKs results from minimizing proof lengths together with the absence of direct user interactions. zk-SNARKs make it possible to execute prover and verifier steps simultaneously within constant time through their single proof verification operation. Blockchain scalability improves through efficiency because maximum processing requirements no longer exist at the individual nodes throughout the network.

zk-SNARKs adoption by Ethereum continues at an increasing pace because they boost privacy and scalability features. Through zk-SNARK integration Ethereum achieves confidential deals with hidden transaction data while maintaining blockchain integrity. Ethereum benefits from zk-SNARKs through its layer-2 network solutions which help improve off-chain transaction processing efficiency and maintain security features and decentralization of the platform.

5 Security Implications

Blockchains built on Ethereum depend mostly on cryptographic security measures to secure their networks. Encryption-based tools ensure robust transaction authentication which remains possible through integration with current security hazards. Blockchain technology depends on cryptographic algorithms to build both safe transactions together with security protocols in order to operate its decentralized trustless system. Security problems rarely develop even when protective systems function yet they require ongoing development with active monitoring.

Blockchain systems experience their biggest security challenge in the form of private keys management. Within Ethereum blockchain each user needs private keys for two core functions which include account identification and asset management control [7]. Permanent asset loss along with security breaches of connected assets result from both private key thefts and loss incidents. Key management solutions prove essential due to ongoing key thefts which cause permanent losses of private storage assets. Users can reinforce their security through hardware wallets together with multi-signature systems but they need protection from private key intrusion attempts and malicious phishers and malware.

Smart contracts feature secure automatic programming but they maintain exposure to bugs in their program code and operational structure flaws. Smart contracts became exposed to numerous risks because of the 2016 DAO hack incident. The exploiter accessed a code vulnerability in the smart contract thus triggering a massive financial loss. Users need to do full testing and formal verification together with independent audits of smart contract logic before deployment because it proves that the logic works properly.

All current cryptographic methods face dangerous future threats because of the emerging quantum computing technology. ECDSA functions today as the main cryptographic protocol but quantum computers demonstrate the threat to break it since classical attacks do not affect this method. The research into post-quantum cryptography represents a necessity for blockchains because they must stay responsive to upcoming modifications in computational strength.

Blockchain security stands on cryptography and demands continued development of protective measures that will safeguard against upcoming security threats in the system.

6 Future Trends and Developments

The speed of cryptographic-blockchain interplay development increases because users require fortified security combined with better scalability and privacy solutions. Blockchain capabilities receive fundamental changes because of several emerging cryptographic methods used by Ethereum and its associated blockchain platforms [8].

PQC stands as the main cryptographic research category because quantum computers present a threat to standard algorithms including ECC used in Ethereum security systems. Scientists persistently search for quantum-resistant algorithms which will defend blockchain systems from being compromised during the arrival of quantum technology. To implement PQC providers must handle its integration process meticulously because the change impacts fundamental blockchain cryptographic methods.

Homomorphic Encryption (HE) represents a promising development since it enables encrypted data processing without data decryption in the system [9]. This technique represents a breakthrough for blockchain privacy because it enables data processing security along with confidentiality maintenance. Smart contracts using HE enable processing confidential data in a secure manner without exposing the information to blockchain networks thus enabling novel privacy-enhanced decentralized applications (dApps).

Active key management systems through Multi-Party Computation (MPC) evolve the security features while preventing private key exposure to unauthorized users. Through MPC different participants resolve a shared function as all entries stay hidden so key theft remains unlikely.

Ethereum 2.0 will bring BLS (Boneh-Lynn-Shacham) signatures during its Proof of Stake (PoS) update to boost energy efficiency and scalability of the network. The continuous development of cryptography within the blockchain presents a dual purpose of technological advancement and solutions for digital age challenges.

7 Conclusion

Trustless decentralized systems in modern digital world operate through a unified power system that unites blockchain technology with cryptography. The necessary blockchain security components which involve hashing and digital signatures with public-key cryptography enable transaction security and maintain blockchain data integrity and prevents modifications. Through its development process Ethereum proves that cryptographic tools equipped with superior capabilities allow users to construct smart contracts together with dApps and secure private features that use zk-SNARKs. Any progress in blockchain depends heavily on Ethereum's addition of Proof of Stake and BLS signatures through its version update. Crypto technological advancements provide both superior system operation along with developing cryptographic needs to fight upcoming computing issues including quantum breakthroughs. The key performance factors of blockchain are dependent on secure private key management and contracted code precision but both areas expose potential human errors in implementation. Achieving a robust connection between blockchain technology and cryptography requires ongoing substantial research together with testing and innovation efforts. The collaboration between these two technological elements drives continuous redesign of decentralized systems because it establishes new digital security standards and privacy protection practices across multiple industries.

Acknowledgments. I would like to express my sincere gratitude to Dr. Tu, whose guidance, wisdom, and unwavering belief in my potential shaped the way I think and engage with the world. I am endlessly grateful for the impact he has left and knowledge he has shared along the way.

Disclosure of Interests. The authors have no competing interests to declare that are relevant to the content of this article.

References

1. Zheng, Z., Xie, S., Dai, H., Chen, X., Wang, H.: An overview of blockchain technology: architecture, consensus, and future trends. In: 2017 IEEE International Congress on Big Data (BigData Congress), pp. 557–564. IEEE (2017)
2. Wang, X.: Blockchain security and applications: A comprehensive analysis from hash functions to consensus algorithms. Theor. Nat. Sci. **31**, 292–298 (2024)
3. Feltovic, M.: From theory to practice: the role of cryptography in securing blockchain networks. MEST J. **12**(2) (2024)
4. Kuznetsov, O., Rusnak, A., Yezhov, A., Kuznetsova, K., Kanonik, D., Domin, O.: Merkle trees in blockchain: a study of collision probability and security implications. Internet Things 101193 (2024)
5. Kumar, N.S., Brinthakumari, S., Partheeban, N.: Navigating the blockchain landscape with a comprehensive survey of smart contracts, ethereum, and consensus mechanisms. In: 2024 4th International Conference on Data Engineering and Communication Systems (ICDECS), pp. 1–6. IEEE (2024)
6. Sah, C.P., Kaur, M., Singh, G.: Efficiency of zero-knowledge proofs: a through review and analysis. In: 2024 IEEE International Conference on Public Key Infrastructure and its Applications (PKIA), pp. 1–7. IEEE (2024)
7. Jamwal, S., Cano, J., Lee, G.M., Tran, N.H., Truong, N.: A survey on ethereum pseudonymity: techniques, challenges, and future directions. J. Netw. Comput. Appl. 104019 (2024)
8. Obaidat, M.A., Rawashdeh, M., Alja'afreh, M., Abouali, M., Thakur, K., Karime, A.: Exploring IoT and blockchain: a comprehensive survey on security, integration strategies, applications and future research directions. Big Data Cogn. Comput **8**(12), 174 (2024)
9. Mollakuqe, E., et al.: Applications of homomorphic encryption in secure computation. Open Res. Eur. **4**(158), 158 (2024)

SecLog: Atomic-Swap Based Secure Logging for Decentralized Data Sharing

Avery Hughes[1], Showkot Hossain[2], Wenyi Tang[2], Taeho Jung[2], and Changhao Chenli[1]([✉])

[1] Indiana Institute of Technology, Fort Wayne, IN 46803, USA
ahughes02@indianatech.net, cchenli@indianatech.edu
[2] University of Notre Dame, Notre Dame, IN 46556, USA
{shossain,wtang3,tjung}@nd.edu

Abstract. Data sharing benefits various aspects of people's daily lives, while in most existing centralized sharing paradigms, data generators do not have the ownership or control over their data. There have been many recent works on decentralized data sharing that provide the data owners with full control over their generated data in a decentralized setting. However, besides guaranteeing the owners with more control over their data, record tracking for data requesters becomes challenging due to the decentralization attribute. To address this issue, we propose SecLog, an atomic-swap based secure logging for decentralized data sharing. We utilized the idea of atomic swap from existing works, modifying the triggered event when the access to the queried results is given to the data requester, a record will be automatically included on the blockchain. Simulation results indicate that our proposed protocol costs less gas compared to the original payment-based atomic swaps and our source code is available at: https://github.com/avocado-avery/SecLog.

Keywords: Decentralized Data Sharing · Secure Logging · Atomic-Swap on Blockchain · Provenance Tracking

1 Introduction

Data sharing has become more and more prevalent as the value of data is continuously increasing. According to a recent report from American Hospital Association's Center for Health Innovations[1], the health care industry is currently leveraging data to improve not only patients' experiences and costs, but also clinical and operational performance. In fact, beyond the health care industry, a huge amount of data is generated every day and usually collected and shared by/among some central parties (e.g., companies, hospitals, data centers, etc.). These shared data, on the one hand, can benefit both product improvements in industry and research progress in academia. On the other hand, however, users who generate these data barely participate in the entire sharing process.

---

[1] https://www.aha.org/center/market-insights/leveraging-data.

ⓒ The Author(s), under exclusive license to Springer Nature Switzerland AG 2026
S. Chen et al. (Eds.): METAVERSE 2025, LNCS 16159, pp. 115–124, 2026.
https://doi.org/10.1007/978-3-032-06323-6_9

In many cases, the only thing that data generators (denoted as "owners" hereafter) know about this process is when they initially sign the agreement for allowing some entity to share their data. After that, the data owners have no clue about the data sharing details, such as who accessed their data, when the data were accessed and how the data were used, etc. Such sharing without transparency also makes the data sharing field incompliant with many existing laws, regulations and acts (e.g., Health Insurance Portability and Accountability Act (HIPAA), General Data Protection Regulation (GDPR), California Consumer Privacy Act (CCPA), etc.).

Many decentralized databases have been proposed[2], which are solutions to address such concerns. In most decentralized data sharing frameworks [8,10,11], data owners have the control over their generated data. Data users (requesters) will send their queries to an API, which will return the query results based on some system defined policy (e.g., access control list etc.). (A detailed description of one of the newest decentralized data sharing frameworks can be found in Sect. 2.3.) Although in such decentralized sharing systems, the ownership and the control of the data are returned back to the data owners, they still lack the ability of tracking the data retrieval/sharing behaviors between the users and the API. However, provenance tracking is necessary for all such data sharing platforms as it can ensure both accountability and traceability for the system, but is very challenging for a decentralized system. Unlike traditional centralized sharing paradigms, in decentralized systems, there is no trusted authority who can keep track of all the behaviors and maintain a centralized copy of logs. How to make sure that when data are successfully retrieved, certain logs will automatically be enforced, is therefore challenging in most current decentralized data sharing systems.

Blockchain is a Distributed Ledger Technology (DLT) which can be used to keep a chain of records without being tampered with under a decentralized setting, and is therefore a very popular data structure for logging systems (summarized in Sect. 2.1). However, directly using blockchain to store the data sharing behaviors cannot guarantee the correctness and the completeness of the logging. This is because for users who want to deny/repudiate the receipt of the retrieved data, they will not confirm with the API that they have received the data. It is not appropriate to let API update the logs because there might be other factors (i.e., network issues) such that the users indeed miss the returned data, which may also cause a single point of failure (SPOF) risk potentially. With this in mind, another line of works on fair exchange (summarized in Section Sect. 2.2) provides us with new ideas on further addressing the secure logging problem in a decentralized data sharing. Fair exchange protocols usually leverage an atomic swap design on top of a blockchain network, where a data buyer will set up a Hashed Timelocked Contract (HTLC) to exchange the access to the data and the payment with the data seller atomically. Although in our problem setting, the user will not pay the API for data retrieval, the atomicity between the access

---

[2] https://github.com/recallnet/awesome-decentralized-database.

to the requested data and some event to be triggered at the same time is a very important property that we want to achieve in our design.

With all the above in mind, we propose SecLog, an Atomic-Swap Based Secure Logging for Decentralized Data Sharing. Our contribution includes: 1) a novel atomic-swap based logging protocol which can enforce logging when some sharing is successfully conducted in a decentralized setting; 2) the system security is also proved; 3) we tested our protocol via simulation and the results indicate that our design consumes less gas compared to the existing payment-based atomic swap protocols; 4) the source code[3] is also released for reproducibility.

The rest of the paper is organized as follows: in Sect. 2 we summarized related works and briefly introduced the Web3DB system as preliminaries. We introduced the detailed system design in Sect. 3. Our simulation results and analysis are summarized in Sect. 4. The paper is concluded in Sect. 5.

2 Related Works and Preliminaries

2.1 Blockchain-Based Logging

Blockchain technologies are now a prevalent tool for making logging more secure and auditable. Numerous solutions exist that are looking to remove central control and offer verifiable proofs, yet still rely on implicit trust with participants. Gao et al. [6] employ homomorphic encryption to secure audit logs on a blockchain, enhancing confidentiality but at the expense of excluding users from being able to verify log inclusion. Cha et al. [1] present an IoT auditing system built on blockchain, although its reliability depends on a trusted infrastructure. Zhao et al. [20] and Lopez-Pimentel et al. [9] store hashes of Merkle tree and root user events on-chain for tamper evidence, but use off-chain storage which is a matter of concern. Hsu et al. [7] combine blockchain and access control for IoT storage, while Cha et al. [1] and Hasan et al. [19] use trusted execution environments to secure cloud logs. AuditChain [17], BlockAuditor [18], and LogChain [12] adopt more decentralized designs but still assume honest participants in the infrastructure and do not address omission attacks, where events may be excluded without detection. Besides, there are other protocols utilizing blockchain to manage and store identity information [14] and supporting tracing/tracking functions using the stored provenance graph on the blockchain [13].

These limitations reflect a broader issue in existing architectures: the absence of mechanisms that allow users to independently confirm that their actions were successfully logged. While current systems [12,17,18] adopt decentralized designs and ensure tamper resistance via blockchain logging, they still assume cooperative infrastructure and do not defend against omission attacks, where events may be silently excluded. While most solutions prioritize immutability and integrity, few offer guarantees of inclusion from the front end user's perspective. To address

---

[3] https://github.com/avocado-avery/SecLog.

this, our approach integrates verification into the logging process, enabling verifiable inclusion and censorship resistance without requiring trusted logger, storage node, or any single participant.

2.2 Fair-Exchange Protocols

Fair-exchange protocols provide a second avenue for verifiable, zero-trust interactions. FairSwap [4], OptiSwap [5], and Universal Atomic Swaps [16] rely on smart contracts and cryptographic primitives for enforcement of atomicity among parties. The exchanges are designed for currency or data exchange and are not intended for use with ongoing, continuous logging. Recent advancements push atomic swap concepts further into the realm of data exchange. Zhu et al. [21] and Tas et al. [15] use private key exchange and zero-knowledge proofs for facilitating fairness among blockchains. They ensure integrity at transfer time but are not persistently audit-proof and do not enable ever-running event checking.

Building on these foundations, our system applies atomicity principles to more than just asset transfer. While there are several protocols [2–5,16] enforce fairness through smart contracts, they focus on single-shot exchanges of data or currency between two parties. Similarly, recent work by Zhu et al. [21] and Tas et al. [15] extends atomicity through private key exchange and zero-knowledge proofs, but their models do not support persistent, auditable event streams.

2.3 Brief Review of Web3DB

Web3DB [10] is a decentralized RDBMS (relational database management system) which can support SQL, aiming to return data control to data owners' (people who generate data), rather than letting data centers take full control over their data. The modularized system consists of four major layers, namely the Data Injection Layer, the Access Control Layer, the Database Engine Layer, and the Data Storage Layer. The Data Storage Layer leverages IPFS (InterPlanetary File System) as their underlying storage protocol. When users would like to interact with the system, they will send their query requests to the SQL API. The API will first talk to the Access Control Layer, where users' credentials will be verified and query requests will be re-written if they are valid according to the ACL (Access Control List). The API will then forward the re-written queries to the Data Engine Layer, where a random selected master node will coordinate all other slave nodes to execute the queries and return the results back to the API after completion. The API will return the results back to users.

3 System Design

3.1 System Model, Security Model and Assumptions

As aforementioned in Sect. 2.3, in Web3DB, users will send query requests to the SQL API, and finally, the API will return the results received from the Database Engine Layer. However, the underlying assumption behind this process is that the users are honest, i.e., they will not deny receiving the results. Such an assumption may not always be practical in an Internet-based environment. On the other hand, this phase involves a two-party data sharing process, which requires secure logging for the purposes of accountability and non-repudiation. Therefore, SecLog will focus on relaxing the assumption of honest users while still guaranteeing a secure logging protocol in Web3DB.

System Model: In SecLog, we consider the following three types of entities, including users, API and blockchain nodes. Users are the entities that send out query requests and wait for retrieving the results from the API. API is the entity in charge of receiving request, collecting results and returning to the corresponding users. The blockchain nodes are those entities maintaining blockchain status, usually by validating transactions and executing smart contract functions.

Note that the discussion of blockchain nodes' misbehaviors is out of the range of this paper, as such concerns are usually resolved or discussed under the field of consensus mechanisms, which is irrelevant to this paper's topic.

Security Model: we consider two properties, namely *correctness* and *completeness* in SecLog, and the definition are given as below:

Definition 1. *Correctness. We say our SecLog is correct if, for any sharing record on the blockchain, the corresponding sharing was indeed finished, which means that the API sent the query results and the user received the queried data.*

Definition 2. *Completeness. We say our SecLog is complete if, for any successful data retrieval, a corresponding record will be included on the blockchain.*

Assumptions: We assume that: (1) the underlying blockchain is secure against consensus-level attacks (e.g., 51% attacks) and nodes will not collude to censor specific transactions (such as the user's contract deployment or the API's contract call). Therefore, its liveness will be guaranteed. This will guarantee that the user will eventually have access to the queried data, as long as they can get online after the API's response has been confirmed by the blockchain. (2) We assume that the queried data will be transmitted with encryption. Otherwise, the data will either be accessed by all nodes on the blockchain or the querier will deny receiving the data. (3) The API may suffer crash faults, whereas Byzantine faults are not considered. In the worst-case scenario, the API may become unresponsive to the users. The discussion of a malicious data provider is out of the range of this paper, and there are many related works [3,4] discussed about data correctness.

3.2   Our Design of SecLog

Now we give out the detailed design of SecLog. As is shown in Fig. 1, after the API retrieves the query results from the Database Engine Layer, the API will first encrypt the query results using its secret key sk. The API will further split its sk into two parts, (sk_1, sk_2) where $sk = sk_1 + sk_2$ (step 1). After that, the

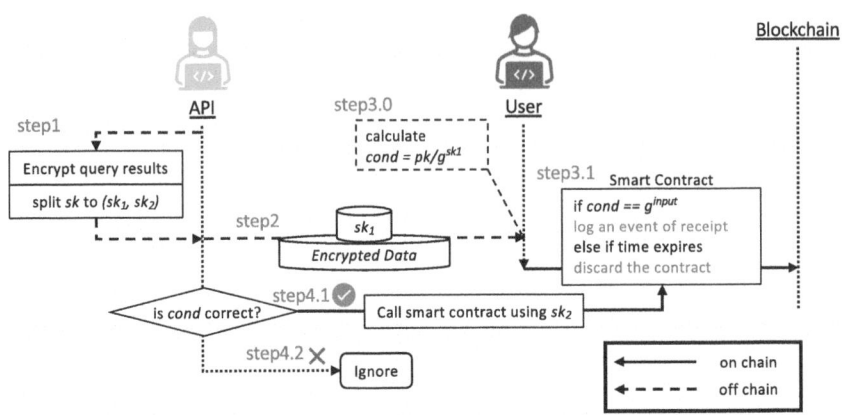

Fig. 1. Workflow of SecLog

API will send both the sk_1 and the encrypted query results to the front end user (step 2). Note that so far, both steps are conducted off-chain, which means sk_1 is a secret value known by the API and the user only. After receiving the encrypted data and sk_1, the user will use sk_1 to calculate a condition value *cond*, where $cond = pk/g^{sk_1}$ (step 3.0). Then, the user will write a smart contract and deploy it onto the blockchain. Namely, the contract will be a variant HTLC (Hashed Timelock Contract), requiring that an event of logging a receipt will be triggered and recorded only when the correct input such that $g^{input} == cond$ is provided. Otherwise, no event will be logged and the contract will be discarded after its expiration time (step 3.1). After the smart contract is deployed onto the blockchain, the API will validate whether the condition *cond* is correctly set. If so, the API will call the smart contract using sk_2 to trigger the receipt logging event (step 4.1). Otherwise, the API will ignore the smart contract (step 4.2).

For details of the *input* verification process, we followed the implementation that was proposed in the Fair^{2}Trade [3]. Specifically, we will also use the ElGamal cryptosystem as an example for our implementation. The API's public key pk is determined by its randomly chosen secret key, sk, where $pk = y^{sk}$ and y is the group generator in ElGamal. As aforementioned, the API will randomly split its sk into two parts, such that $sk = sk_1 + sk_2$, and send sk_1 to the user. After receiving sk_1, the user will calculate the required *input* such that $g^{input} = pk/g^{sk_1}$. Note that since $pk = g^{sk}$, we then have $pk/g^{sk_1} = g^{sk}/g^{sk_1} = g^{sk-sk_1} = g^{sk_2}$. Therefore, as long as the API provide the correct sk_2, the user will be able to recover sk and decrypt the ciphertext, while the event of the user successfully redeemed the query results will also be automatically triggered and logged. Since our major contribution is on logging enforcement instead of the *input* verification, we cannot include the complete description and corresponding security analysis due to the page limit, and we sincerely invite interested readers to read the original design proposed in [3].

3.3   Security Analysis

With the detailed description of the SecLog, we now prove that our design of SecLog can guarantee both *correctness* and *completeness*.

Theorem 1. *The proposed design of SecLog guarantees correctness, as long as the user can access the blockchain at least once after the API's response is confirmed by the blockchain.*

Proof. The proof is straightforward. If the user has a stable access to the network, they can recover sk as soon as the API provides the correct sk_2. The special case is that some user may get disconnected from the network, and cannot get updates from the blockchain in a timely manner. However, as we assumed before Sect. 3.1, the liveness of the underlying blockchain is guaranteed. That means after the API's input is confirmed by the blockchain, as long as the user can get a connection to network and receive updates from the blockchain once, they will be able to access the sk_2 and finally retrieve the query results. This proves the correctness of SecLog.

Theorem 2. *The proposed design of SecLog guarantees completeness, as long as the API provides a valid input to a valid smart contract deployed by the user.*

Proof. The proof is similar to that of Theorem 1. In fact, according to the atomic attribute of the HTLC, when a correct *input* was provided, blockchain nodes will validate the *input* and execute the event of logging afterwards. Therefore, as long as the smart contract is correctly deployed, a valid *input* will always trigger the corresponding logging event, which guarantees that record will be included on the blockchain.

4   Evaluation and Analysis

4.1   Evaluation and Experiments

As aforementioned, the design of SecLog followed the idea from Fair^{2}Trade [3], which utilizes a variant of HTLC to realize atomic exchange. Briefly speaking, in Fair^{2}Trade, a data buyer will setup an HTLC and the data broker will redeem the deposit in the contract by providing the access to the data. As described in Sect. 3.2, we let the front end users serve as the data buyer and take the API as the broker. To test SecLog's performance, we implemented our protocol using smart contract on Ethereum and conducted a gas cost measurement using Truffle and a local Ganache blockchain. Besides comparing our final design, `Seclog.sol` with the original Fair^{2}Trade's work, `Fair²Trade.sol`, we further came up with another naïve benchmark, `CIDLog.sol`, for comparison. Instead of encrypting the query results first and providing the other half of the decryption keys to the HTLC, in CIDLog's design, the API will store the query results to IPFS, and take the CID of the results as the sk to exchange with the user using HTLC. All three contracts were compiled and deployed with Solidity 0.5.0, with gas usage collected directly from logs in Ganache and Truffle's console.

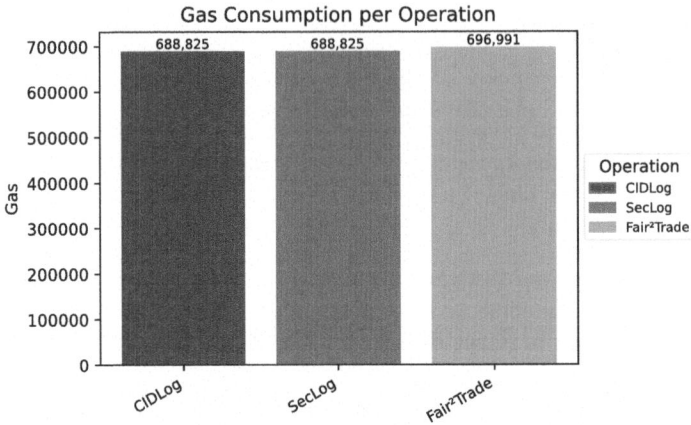

Fig. 2. Gas consumption per smart contract operation.

The gas consumption results are shown in Fig. 2. The cost difference between SecLog and Fair^{2}Trade is 8,000 gas, where SecLog consumes less gas. This is because in Fair^{2}Trade, after the broker provides a valid sk_2, a payment of transferring the deposit to the broker will be launched. In SecLog, however, only an event of confirming the receipt of a valid *input* will be triggered. Note that although in SecLog a deposit transfer is not triggered, the extra confirmation operation will also cost some gas. This further explains why the cost difference between SecLog and Fair^{2}Trade is less than an ETH transfer, which usually costs 21,000 gas. As for the smart contract in CIDLog, the gas consumption is the same as that of SecLog, because the length of CID is the same as the length of the sk (both 32 bytes). The overall costs among all three contracts are close, this is because the major gas consumption comes from the Elliptic Curve calculation for the sk/CID verification. However, in CIDLog, the user cannot download the data until the atomic swap is completed, which will introduce one more entity (e.g., an IPFS node) into the system, and hence increases the difficulty of data verification. According to etherscan[4], as of 7/26/2025, the execution of SecLog will cost around \$0.75, which further indicates that our protocol is financially affordable in real-world scenarios.

4.2   Discussion and Analysis

According to the design of SecLog, besides the extra procedure of smart contract deployment and calling introduced to the users and the API, there are some additional cost introduced as well. On the one hand, users need to interact with the blockchain network to receive the *input* from the API, which may increase the network burden and have extra requirements on the users' network service quality. Moreover, the frequency for users to stay synced with the most

---

[4] https://etherscan.io/gastracker.

recent record may vary based on the underlying blockchain. (E.g., Bitcoin's block interval is around 10 min while Ethereum's is approximately 12 s.) On the other hand, the blockchain usage will also introduce extra cost for its maintenance, although the liveness of the blockchain was assumed in Sect. 3.1. However, the choice of the underlying blockchain will be determined by the exact system implementation, which means the maintenance cost of using blockchain may also change. Besides these, there might be other off-chain overhead such as data encryption/decryption and key splitting. For instance, it takes less than 10 ms to encrypt a 1 MB payload using AES encryption, and key splitting can be completed within 1 ms, both of which are much smaller compared to the on-chain overhead.

5   Conclusion

In this paper, we propose SecLog, an atomic-swap based secure logging for decentralized data sharing. The core design of our proposed protocol utilizes the idea from the existing atomic swap works. Specifically, we modify the implementation of HTLC that, when a correct *input* is provided, instead of launching a payment transfer, an event will be triggered and recorded to the blockchain indicating that a data retrieval succeeds. We also run a simulation to test SecLog's performance, and the results show that compared to the benchmark work of payment-based atomic swap, our gas consumption is lower.

Acknowledgment. This work is partially sponsored by NASA ULI under Grant No. 80NSSC23M0058, NSF under Grant No. OAC-2312973.

References

1. Cha, J.-H., Kim, Y.-S., Kim, S.-H.: A blockchain-enabled iot auditing management system complying with iso/iec 15408-2. Sensors **23**(4), 9031 (2023)
2. Chenli, C., Tang, W., Jung, T.: Fairtrade: efficient atomic exchange-based fair exchange protocol for digital data trading. In: 2021 IEEE Blockchain, pp. 38–46. IEEE (2021)
3. Chenli, C., Tang, W., Lee, H., Jung, T.: Fair^{2}trade: digital trading platform ensuring exchange and distribution fairness. IEEE Trans. Depend. Secure Comput. **21**(5), 4827–4842 (2024)
4. Dziembowski, S., Eckey, L., Faust, S.: Fairswap: how to fairly exchange digital goods. In: CCS, pp. 967–984. ACM (2018)
5. Eckey, L., Faust, S., Schlosser, B.: Optiswap: fast optimistic fair exchange. In: ASIA CCS '20, pp. 543–557 (2020)
6. Gao, L.: Enterprise internal audit data encryption based on blockchain technology. PLoS ONE **20**(1), e0315759 (2025)
7. Hsu, C.-L., Chen, W.-X., Le, T.-V.: An autonomous log storage management protocol with blockchain mechanism and access control for the internet of things. Sensors **20**(22), 6471 (2020)

8. IceFireDB Team IceFireLabs. Database storage and retrieval protocol built for web3.0. https://www.icefiredb.xyz/
9. López-Pimentel, J.C., Morales-Rosales, L.A., Monroy, R.: RootLogChain: registering log-events in a blockchain for audit issues from the creation of the root. Sensors **21**(22), 7669 (2021)
10. Mukherjee, S.S., et al.: Web3db: Web 3.0 rdbms for individual data ownership. arXiv:2504.02713 (2025)
11. Orbitdb. Orbitdb/orbitdb: Peer-to-peer databases for the decentralized web. https://github.com/orbitdb/orbitdb
12. Pourmajidi, W., Miranskyy, A.: Logchain: blockchain-assisted log storage. arXiv:1805.08868 (2018)
13. Tang, W., Chenli, C., Ju, C., Jung, T.: Trac2chain: trackability and traceability of graph data in blockchain with linkage privacy. In: Proceedings of the 37th ACM/SIGAPP Symposium on Applied Computing, pp. 272–281 (2022)
14. Tang, W., et al.: Grac: graph-based anonymous credentials from identity graphs on blockchain. In: 2024 IEEE International Conference on Blockchain (Blockchain), pp. 113–122. IEEE (2024)
15. Tas, E.N., et al.: Atomic and fair data exchange via blockchain. In: CCS '24, pp. 3227–3241 (2024)
16. Thyagarajan, S.A.K., Malavolta, G., Moreno-Sanchez, P.: Universal atomic swaps: secure exchange of coins across all blockchains. In: 2022 IEEE (SP), pp. 1299–1316. IEEE (2022)
17. Vishnia, G., Peters, G.W.: Auditchain: a trading audit platform over blockchain. Front. Blockchain **3**, 9 (2020)
18. Xu, S., Ning, J., Ma, J., Huang, X., Deng, R.H.: K-time modifiable and epoch-based redactable blockchain. IEEE Trans. Inf. Forensics Secur. **16**, 4507–4520 (2021)
19. Zawoad, S., Dutta, A.K., Hasan, R.: Seclaas: secure logging-as-a-service for cloud forensics. In: ASIA CCS '13, pp. 219–230. ACM (2013)
20. Zhao, W., Aldyaflah, I.M., Gangwani, P., Joshi, S., Upadhyay, H., Lagos, L.: A blockchain-facilitated secure sensing data processing and logging system. IEEE Access **11**, 3252030 (2023)
21. Zhu, Z., Zhang, R., Tao, Y.: Atomic cross-chain swap based on private key exchange. Cybersecurity **7**(1), 1–19 (2024)

Author Index

© The Editor(s) (if applicable) and The Author(s), under exclusive license
to Springer Nature Switzerland AG 2026
S. Chen et al. (Eds.): METAVERSE 2025, LNCS 16159, p. 125, 2026.
https://doi.org/10.1007/978-3-032-06323-6

The manufacturer's authorised representative in the EU is Springer
Nature Customer Service Centre GmbH, Europaplatz 3, 69115 Heidelberg,
Germany. If you have any concerns regarding our products, please
contact ProductSafety@springernature.com

Printed and bound by CPI Group (UK) Ltd, Croydon, CR0 4YY

29/04/2026

02099511-0010